ess to
hip

Other titles in the Access to the Curriculum series

Access to History
Curriculum Planning and Practical Activities for Pupils with Learning Difficulties
Andrew Turner
£14.00
1 85346 857 6
March 2002

Access to Science
Curriculum Planning and Practical Activities for Pupils with Learning Difficulties
Claire Marvin and Chris Stokoe
£14.00
1 85346 917 3
April 2003

Related titles

Practical Resources for Teaching Citizenship in Secondary Classrooms
David Leddington and Ruth Tudor
£15.00
1 85346 840 1
July 2002

Teaching Citizenship in the Secondary School
James Arthur and Daniel Wright
£17.00
1 85346 744 8
July 2001

Access to Citizenship

Curriculum planning and practical activities for pupils with learning difficulties

Ann Fergusson and Hazel Lawson

David Fulton Publishers
London

David Fulton Publishers Ltd
The Chiswick Centre, 414 Chiswick High Road, London W4 5TF

www.fultonpublishers.co.uk

David Fulton Publishers is a division of Granada Learning Ltd, part of the Granada Media group.

First published in Great Britain in 2003 by David Fulton Publishers
10 9 8 7 6 5 4 3 2 1

Note: The right of Ann Fergusson and Hazel Lawson to be identified as the authors of this work has been asserted by them in accordance with the Copyright, Designs and Patents Act 1988.

British Library Cataloguing in Publication Data
A catalogue record for this book is available from the British Library.

ISBN 1–85346–910–6

Typeset by FiSH Books, London
Printed and bound in Great Britain by Ashford Colour Press Limited, Gosport, Hants

Contents

Acknowledgements

We wish to thank the following schools for their contributions:

Critchill School, Frome, Somerset

Emily Fortey School, Leicester

Jack Taylor School, London

Kingsley School, Kettering, Northamptonshire

Lakeside School, Welwyn Garden City

Marshfields School, Peterborough

Meldreth Manor School, Royston, Hertfordshire

Montacute School, Poole

St George's School, Peterborough

Sunfield School, Clent, Stourbridge

Watling View School, St Albans, Hertfordshire

Institute for Citizenship, for permission to use extracts from *Citizenship Education for Young People with Special Educational Needs*:
- Rap (p. 74)
- Different ways of voting for party (p. 85)
- The platypus story (p. 73)
- Questions about adverts (p. 87)
- Practising meetings (p. 94)
- Starter ideas for school councils (p. 99)

Logotron for symbols from the Mayer-Johnson PCS Symbols and Rebus collection

Kogan Page for Marshfields School extract.

Finally, thanks to our families – Callum and Derek Shea and Niall, Dale and Keith Lawson.

Foreword

'I am a citizen, not of Athens or Greece, but of the world.'

Socrates 469–399 BC

The sentiments expressed by Socrates in recognising that he had responsibilities which went beyond those to his immediate countrymen may possibly have a greater resonance in today's society than when they were expressed by the great teacher and philosopher. As more people have the ability to travel and visit other cultures, and in an age when images from across the world enter our homes through the media and, increasingly, the internet, we become more aware of the fact that we are part of a relatively small planet and that our own actions can have an impact upon people who we have never met, and are unlikely ever to meet.

For the individual living at home but regularly confronted by images of other people, many of them living in distressing conditions or subjected to violence, poverty or abuse, it is difficult not to become inured or to be overwhelmed by the magnitude of difficulties which confront so many within the global population. However, if we take Socrates at his word, there is an alternative approach, which demands that we accept our duty to act responsibly as citizens and work in collaboration with others for greater social justice and the common good. In placing a new emphasis upon Citizenship within the curriculum, the UK government has taken an important step in enabling teachers to assist pupils to learn more about themselves and their responsibilities to the communities in which they live.

These changes to the curriculum must be embraced by *all* teachers for *all* pupils if they are to have the impact which is intended. It is insufficient for politicians and other leaders, including teachers, to make statements about the need to develop a more equitable society unless these are supported by positive actions. In May 2002 the United Nations General Assembly invited 404 young people from around the world to attend a conference and express their views about issues which concerned them. The eloquence with which they articulated their opinions was matched only by the compassion they demonstrated for children around the world. During this assembly they presented the following statement:

> We are the world's children.
> We are the victims of exploitation and abuse.
> We are street children.
> We are the children of war.
> We are the victims and orphans of HIV/AIDS.
> We are denied good-quality education and health care.
> We are victims of political, economic, cultural, religious and environmental discrimination.
> We are children whose voices are not being heard: it is time we were taken into account.

The new importance attached to Citizenship within the curriculum provides an important opportunity to ensure that the next generation of policy-makers and leaders have an increased awareness of their responsibilities which enable them to make better decisions than their predecessors. However, at a time when educational inclusion is rightly at the forefront of the international educational agenda it is essential that we ensure that access to good teaching in relation to citizenship becomes an entitlement of all pupils.

Hazel Lawson and Ann Fergusson bring a wealth of experience to this book which should ensure that teachers of pupils with special educational needs are well supported in providing exciting opportunities for their pupils. Throughout this text they have demonstrated an empathic approach to understanding the many challenges which confront teachers working with an often challenging group of pupils. The ideas they present are both practical and grounded in a sound theoretical base and understanding of the issues of teaching and learning in relation to pupils for whom the acquisition and retention of knowledge, skills and understanding is seldom easily achieved. In considering the content of what might be taught to pupils they have clearly reflected upon recent QCA guidance which suggests that citizenship begins with pupils learning about themselves and understanding their relationship to others. They have, however, moved beyond this in recognising that all pupils, regardless of need or ability, have much to offer to the communities in which they live and to a wider society.

This book is timely in addressing an area which is presenting new challenges to teachers and new opportunities for all pupils. The advice contained within is supported by a pragmatic approach to enabling pupils to participate fully in learning activities from which they will benefit, but also the society in which they will live. In so doing this book makes a positive contribution to the bid for greater inclusion.

Richard Rose
Centre for Special Needs Education and Research
University College Northampton

Preface

This book has arisen from a passion that has evolved as a result of our work on Citizenship and Personal Social and Health Education (PSHE) with other practitioners in the field of learning difficulties. As we have become more familiar with the very 'essence' of this area, we have developed an increasing belief that citizenship is so much about inclusion, a force to drive it forward. What is so exciting is that the principles by which citizenship demands to be addressed are the very principles that we hold and prioritise for our students with learning difficulties.

In our current climate, where pressures are on performance measurement, citizenship, together with PSHE, requires that we 'return to first principles' by employing interactive and flexible approaches to meet the diverse needs of our students, by truly involving them not just in the learning process, but also the living process. High profile is given to active participation, relationships and a sense of belonging, where attitudes and values are positive and shared by all in the life and work of the school and beyond. Success in addressing Citizenship education will provide the same, firm footing necessary for effective and meaningful learning for pupils, particularly those at the earliest stages of development, in all areas of education and inclusion.

There are strong links with PSHE throughout, despite the emphasis being on Citizenship. Indeed, PSHE and citizenship may perhaps be viewed as most meaningful when considered jointly. In taking this view we may be able to offer greater access, particularly for those students who are at the earliest levels of learning and functioning. By focusing on the very familiar personal experiences of our young people, their responses and their ability to have an effect on their lives, we are more likely to create learning experiences that are meaningful, and, hopefully, transferable.

Citizenship is therefore an important area for individuals throughout their lifelong learning. For this reason we have used the terms 'pupils' and 'students' interchangeably, to include learners of all ages. While recognising that much of the context that we discuss here is to do with the school and the curriculum, the philosophy and, indeed, many of the approaches and activities are strikingly appropriate for individuals with learning disabilities beyond the school setting.

This book seeks to explore this 'essence', to discover what citizenship is and, in particular, what it means for students with learning difficulties. We hope to unravel the necessary content, contexts and approaches to address this area, and to enable and empower our students as successful and active citizens.

We have endeavoured to offer a balance of background, theory and practical suggestions that inform each other. What we also hope is that we inspire professional reflection and challenge to practice.

CHAPTER ONE

The citizenship context

Introduction

The challenge of compiling this book provides us with an exciting opportunity to offer a comprehensive examination of Citizenship – to explore the overall perspective; to scrutinise the theory, politics, relevant literature and background of this area; and to set it within the context of citizenship education and learning difficulties.

Background: The citizenship curriculum

> Schools are always concerned, intentionally or otherwise, with political learning. The ways in which teachers manage classrooms, the respect that pupils have for rules, regulations and for each other, and many other features of what may be termed the hidden curriculum as well as the overtly political nature of what is studied, means that schools will always be one of the key locations for education for citizenship. (Davies 1996: 116)

Citizenship as a curriculum area is not a new concept. Davies (1996) describes some of the background from the 1970s and 1980s and Lawton (2000) traces an interest in citizenship education back to the nineteenth century.

In 1990, as a development of the National Curriculum, introduced in 1988, *Curriculum Guidance 8: Education for Citizenship* (National Curriculum Council 1990) was published as one of five cross-curricular themes. However, along with the other cross-curricular themes (careers education and guidance; education for economic and industrial understanding; health education; and environmental education) it was not supported or resourced and was conceptually at odds with the main body of the National Curriculum. Thus, as Potter (2002) acknowledges, 'Citizenship as a cross-curricular theme was dead in the water from the moment it was launched, in spite of the imaginative efforts of a minority of schools to make something of it' (p. 20).

Through the late 1990s, a number of advisory groups emerged to develop and clarify thinking in this area. These included groups on sustainable development, personal health and social education, careers education, environmental education, the work-related curriculum and one on Citizenship. This National Advisory Group on Citizenship, led by Bernard Crick, produced its report in 1998 *Education for Citizenship and the Teaching of Democracy in Schools* (QCA 1998) and it was Citizenship, rather than any of the other areas, which became a statutory subject within the National Curriculum. There is inevitably, and clearly, a **P**olitical and **p**olitical context for this inclusion of Citizenship as a statutory subject. Rates of drug use, teenage pregnancy, disaffection, crime and truancy among young people were higher than many other countries; voting patterns among young people indicated apathy; there appeared to be a lack of political participation; and issues of equal opportunities, racism and cultural diversity were to the fore, particularly in the wake of the Macpherson Report (1999).

Citizenship curriculum or citizenship education: values, aims, purposes

A statement of agreed values from the National Forum for Values in Education and the Community is included within the National Curriculum handbooks for teachers (DfEE/QCA 1999a; DfEE/QCA 1999b):

The self

We value ourselves as unique human beings capable of spiritual, moral, intellectual and physical growth and development.

Relationships

We value others for themselves, not only for what they have or what they can do for us. We value relationships as fundamental to the development and fulfilment of ourselves and others, and to the good of the community.

Society

We value truth, freedom, justice, human rights, the rule of law and collective effort for the common good. In particular, we value families as sources of love and support for all their members, and as the basis of society in which people care for others.

The environment

We value the environment, both natural and shaped by humanity, as the basis of life and a source of wonder and inspiration.

Drawn from DfEE/QCA 1999a: 148–9

These agreed societal values clearly form a strong basis for citizenship in schools. The stated aims for the school curriculum also explicitly contribute and relate to citizenship:

- 'The school curriculum should aim to provide opportunities for all pupils to learn and achieve
- The school curriculum should aim to promote pupils' spiritual, moral, social and cultural development and prepare all pupils for the opportunities, responsibilities and experiences of life'

(DfEE/QCA 1999a: 11)

As part of the first aim, it is noted that the school curriculum should 'contribute to the development of pupils' sense of identity', 'enable pupils . . . to make a difference for the better' and 'equip them for their future lives as workers and citizens'. Expansion of the second aim includes, for example, 'principles for distinguishing between right and wrong', 'knowledge, understanding and appreciation of their own and different beliefs and cultures', and 'awareness and understanding of, and respect for, the environments in which they live'.

The National Curriculum also establishes an entitlement for all 'to develop knowledge, understanding, skills and attitudes necessary for their self-fulfilment and development as active and responsible citizens' (DfEE/QCA 1999a: 12). Formalisation of Citizenship as a discrete and *statutory* subject at Key Stages 3 and 4 means there will be greater support for teachers and a clearer entitlement for students. At Key Stages 1 and 2, however, *non-statutory* guidelines are provided for PSHE and Citizenship. Some commentators, for example Claire (2001), suggest this is positive and may enable a 'transformative curriculum'. She argues that this non-statutory status might provide a space for more creative teaching and 'for rethinking aspects of the primary curriculum, moving beyond its increasingly technicist instrumental approaches, and acknowledging that education should be about values, empowerment and feelings, as well as numeracy, literacy and preparation for work' (p. 8). However, there is a danger that being non-statutory may give the curriculum area less status and marginalise it at these key stages.

It is also difficult to resolve a contradiction between the government's regulation of schools, the curriculum, target-setting and the drive for standards with their implicit demand for tighter structures and control and the qualities required for the promotion of active citizenship within a school.

For pupils with learning difficulties, it is important to have a view of the citizenship curriculum from two angles, as proposed by Lawson *et al.* (2001). First, we should examine the National Curriculum content – programmes of study for Key Stages 3 and 4 and the non-statutory guidelines for Key Stages 1 and 2 – then adapt, interpret and extend them to make them relevant and appropriate. Secondly, and perhaps more importantly, we should consider what citizenship *is*, what it means, for pupils with learning difficulties. As Jerome and Newman Turner (2001: 55) state:

> Consideration of appropriate learning for students with severe learning difficulties forces us to develop a view of the fundamental aims and principles of the subject which may become more apparent when some of the detail of content and knowledge is stripped away.

When considered in this way, citizenship is envisaged as more than a programme of content and provides opportunities for enabling and empowerment. It then, perhaps, can be viewed as *citizenship education* rather than a citizenship curriculum. This relates well to McGoughlin's (1992) models of minimalist and maximalist approaches to citizenship education (cited in Claire 2001). The minimalist model sees citizenship as informing pupils about their public duty and about the representative processes. A maximalist model, alternatively, views citizenship education as empowerment, where students learn to take responsibility for their own lives and learn how to influence and participate. It is surely this latter model which is most appropriate and desirable for students with learning difficulties, though viewing citizenship in this way inevitably has implications for schools. As Brown (2000: 116) suggests, 'Schools which view citizenship as more than an additional aspect of the formal curriculum will need to review their [own] structures and organisation.'

Defining 'citizens'

Adult citizens

One of the overall aims of citizenship education is to produce active and responsible adult citizens. Diverse definitions of 'citizen' create different perceptions which may exclude people with learning difficulties. For example, Law's (2000) conception of citizenship is similar to some definitions of adulthood in that being a citizen encompasses a number of roles – work role, consumer role, social role and domestic role. Griffiths (1994), similarly, suggests that adult status entails:

- personal autonomy (full responsibility for one's own life);
- productive activity (economic self-sufficiency);
- social interaction and community participation (taking an adult role in society);
- roles within the family (being a non-dependent son or daughter, a spouse or a parent).

What does this mean for students with learning difficulties who may not achieve such levels of autonomy and independence? What roles do they play as adult citizens? As Walmsley (1991: 220) states, 'Citizenship, as it has traditionally been conceived, has seemed an impossible status for people with learning difficulties.' Walmsley noted that people with learning difficulties 'are often confined to the private world of the family' and are excluded from full participation in the community. This, he suggested, was partly through lack of the means by which to exercise their citizenship – 'lack of transport, lack of information and indeed lack of confidence to attend meetings and exercise political rights' (p. 226) – and partly through poverty, as many people with learning difficulties are excluded from paid work and dependent on state benefits. His observations were made more than a decade ago. In that time, citizen-advocacy and self-advocacy groups have emerged, and much ground has been covered in the move toward equality and acceptance of people with learning disabilities. *Valuing People* (DoH 2001), a recent Department of Health report, is the first government initiative to focus on people with learning disabilities for 30 years and has already proved innovative in this crusade.

There is still much work to be done, however, and changes to be made towards a more inclusive society. Progressive concepts of citizenship are still required that positively include people with learning difficulties.

Children as citizens

Historically, childhood has been seen as a 'stage of preparation for adulthood' (Verhellen 2000). Children were seen as 'not yets'. Children were regarded as needing to have their needs met, being looked after and protected, rather than having their rights upheld (Roche 1999).

Alternatively, we may consider that children should be viewed as citizens now, rather than being citizens-in-waiting. Following from the United Nations Convention on the Rights of the Child (1989) there is much greater recognition of children's rights. Article 23 of Convention specifically concerns the rights for children who have disabilities and learning difficulties. It states that children should

> enjoy a full and decent life, in conditions which ensure dignity, promote self-reliance and facilitate the child's active participation in the community... and that the child achieves the fullest possible social integration and individual development. (United Nations 1989, Article 23)

This Convention can be outlined, Verhellen (2000) suggests, as the '3 Ps': protection, provision and participation. Children have the right to be protected from those with greater power; the right to the provision of information, health, education; and the right to participate, to express an opinion. Verhellen goes further: 'These participation rights recognise children as meaning-makers and acknowledge their citizenship' (*ibid.*, p. 35). This is reflected in the view of citizenship apparent in the National Curriculum. It is not just about preparing students to become active citizens as adults; it is also recognising that they are part of society today (Klein 2001).

Miller (1997: 5) lists basic principles with regard to young children taking decisions and being given responsibility:

- 'children have a right to be treated with the same respect as adults;
- children's feelings are as strong and valid as adults';
- children know what is important to them and have the right to express their views and be listened to;
- children's learning is active and relies on being given the opportunity to practise and develop their skills, knowledge and understanding. They will learn to participate by being given the opportunity to do so . . .'

This requires, she continues, that adults provide opportunities for young children to express their views, listen to what children say and take these views into account.

What are the implications of the above for children and young people with learning difficulties, where their levels of development actually cause others to often view and treat them as much younger than their chronological age? We would advocate that our students, regardless of their age or level of development, should have an entitlement to the rights Miller lists, as should very young children.

Power and control

Verhellen's '3 Ps', when considered within the context of learning difficulties, present us with challenges:

- **Protection** (from those with greater power): protection from overt cruelty or physical violence to children in our society may be viewed as unnecessary, but power can take a far more subtle form within education or society generally. Individuals with learning difficulties are particularly vulnerable to all forms of cruelty or abuse.
- **Provision**: children with severe and profound and multiple learning difficulties have only been entitled to receive an education since the Education Act 1970, having, prior to this, been considered 'ineducable'. Since the introduction of the National Curriculum in the late 1980s they have been entitled to the National Curriculum as part of a whole curriculum.
- **Participation**: pupils with special educational needs are considered, by definition, to be 'in need'. It is perhaps this element where a notion of citizenship that acknowledges their right to participation can contribute most. This links with 'protection', as it may challenge power assumptions. It may ensure greater provision to enable more equal access, for example, to the voting system, and thus also relate to 'provision'.

The issue of power and control is an important one. Roche (1999) discusses this in relation to children's rights as citizens, suggesting that adults have to be prepared to give up power. He goes on, 'It is also about recognising the interconnectedness of our lives as adults, parents and children and no longer seeing the relationships between adult and child as naturally and necessarily hierarchic' (p. 485).

Klein (2001) also found that, in order for primary school children to *experience* as well as *learn about* rights, there are implications for power and control in the classroom. She asks:

How do you, as a teacher, loosen the reins that are part and parcel of ensuring structured . . . [curricula and learning environments] . . . How do you allow children to share the responsibility of holding those reins by giving them the right to say what they want to learn and how they want to learn it? (p. vi)

She continues, later in her book:

> [Teachers] had to believe in the children if the children were to believe in themselves, and this could only happen if the teachers were prepared to take risks. It meant them loosening some of their control and allowing children to take the lead sometimes. (p. 32)

The historical evolution of hierarchy in schools is interesting to examine (Brown 2000). Challenging and changing these hierarchical and power relationships can be viewed as 'risky', yet, Brown argues, 'the application of citizenship education will challenge the nature of existing relationships' (p. 116). Holden and Clough (1998: 16) talk of the implications for teachers in needing to examine personally 'the values they hold, the freedom and autonomy they give their pupils, and the choices they make within the curriculum'.

The challenge, then, is to the traditional role and definition of 'teaching' as the imparting of knowledge, something that is 'done to' pupils within the boundaries of established roles and status. This altered perspective on teaching has the emphasis firmly on empowerment and participation. The implications for teachers working with students with learning difficulties are, perhaps, more challenging as the power differential between them may also be greater (Sebba *et al.* 1993).

Enabling or protecting?

Claire (2001) suggests that there are a number of issues which are avoided in the primary PSHE and citizenship guidelines – for example homophobia and bereavement. She argues that such issues are already part of many children's lives at primary age and ought to be included and discussed. She questions whether we are sheltering and protecting children rather than facing up to the real challenge of dealing with this appropriately and meaningfully. We might ask ourselves if we operate in this way with students with learning difficulties. For example, in assuming complexity of conceptualisation of some issues, do we deny pupils empowerment and, unintentionally, shelter and protect rather than enable?

Participation

How then do we encourage active participation? It is only by 'doing citizenship' that students can be effective as 'active participating citizens' of the school (Claire 2001: 107).

One approach, explored fully in Chapter 6 of the present book, is that of school councils. It has been argued that school councils are important, but not sufficient, and they are often 'less democratic in practice than in rhetoric' (*ibid.*: 107). There is much scope here for development in schools and for involving pupils, and this needs to be built into the ethos and democratic practices of the classroom and school – for example through cooperative work or circle time.

It is this active and 'real' involvement and ownership that enables and empowers students. ' "Doing citizenship" implies that you are actively involved in issues and feel you can make a difference through your participation.' (*ibid.*: 108) The implications, Claire explains, are that you have the 'personal confidence and skills to organise your ideas, to talk in public, to listen and debate rationally' (p. 110).

How can such skills be developed in students with learning difficulties? Active participation is partly to do with having a 'voice' and a sense of agency. This requires us to give students a voice; to enable students' views, opinions and expressions, and to listen to these. Additionally, we are responsible for providing curricular opportunities where pupils are given a voice and where their actions can make a difference. Practical applications are addressed further in Chapter 4.

An alternative approach of 'assisted participation' is proposed by Holden and Clough (1998). They liken this to 'assisted performance' based on a social constructivist view of the learning process and drawing on the theoretical perspectives of Vygotsky and Bruner. Social constructivists maintain that through interaction with a more knowledgeable 'other', a child's level of skill and understanding can be enhanced. Less dependence on 'supportive scaffolding' of this type is the desired learning outcome, leading to a greater degree of skill and understanding where external assistance has become unnecessary.

This seems applicable to pupils with learning difficulties who may need assistance in order to participate. Holden and Clough go on to suggest three steps in assisted participation:

- **considering the responses of children and the effect of this on the ethos and culture of the school.** They examine two continua, passive–active and positive–negative, and ask whether we want children who are positive and yet passive, or positive and active?
- **preparing for citizenship, helping pupils to become 'action competent'.** They argue, 'A pupil who is action competent is one who can argue, can reflect critically, can relate her opinions and action to a values framework' (p. 78). Otherwise, they suggest, participation is at a superficial level. They contend that participation alone does not necessarily lead to competent citizens – 'action competence must be developed before participation can be effective' (p. 19). This concept of action competence is difficult to interpret for pupils with learning difficulties in the wider sense, but what we can aim for is competence within familiar contexts in the first instance.
- **consideration of the level of participation.** This issue is one of constant concern, especially in trying to prevent tokenism when working with students at the earliest stages of development. Holden and Clough use an interesting model to look at different levels of participation – Hart's (1992) ladder of participation. Klein (2001) and Miller (1997) also draw upon this ladder. This model explores our concerns in a structured way, although as it is based on mainstream practice, some terminology has a different interpretation to that which has developed in the learning difficulties field.

The ladder describes the following levels of participation:

1. **manipulation** – here pupils may be doing or saying what adults wish them to, but with no real understanding of the issues. Miller provides this example: 'Children are asked to make drawings of an ideal playground. Adults collect the ideas and produce a design for the playground but the children have no idea how their ideas were used and no analysis of the ideas suggested is undertaken' (Miller 1997: 7).
2. **decoration** – here pupils take part in an event but are not given an explanation of the issues. For example, 'Children are asked to wear a T-shirt promoting an issue, or to sing and dance at an event but have little idea of the purpose of the event and no say at all in its organisation' (Miller 1997: 7).
3. **tokenism** – here children have an apparent voice, but have little choice or say in organising the occasion. This notion of tokenism is well known in the field of

working with pupils with learning difficulties, but, as previously stated, has a different interpretation here.

4. **assigned but informed participation** – children understand the intentions of the project, know who made the decisions, volunteer to participate and have a meaningful role.
5. **consulted and informed**
6. **adult-initiated, shared decisions with children.** Miller's example is: 'An environment project to design a park for multi-purpose use involved a group of children and young people to develop the priorities and the design issues. The children produced a range of different models which were then exposed to local community members for comment and modification before being finalised' (Miller 1997: 7).
7. **child-initiated and directed** – the original idea and implementation derive from the children. For example: 'A group of children decide to develop a project to raise money for a charitable cause. They identify the charity, decide the strategy for raising money, organise the necessary activities, collect the money and send it to the charity' (Miller 1997: 7).
8. **child-initiated, shared decisions with adults**

Hart contends that genuine participation does not commence until level 4 (cited in Holden and Clough 1998). Applying this to settings with students with learning difficulties is interesting and demanding of reflection on our practice. However, it is acknowledged that 'it is not necessary that children should always operate at the highest level: different levels are appropriate at different times, depending on the *ability of the child* and the situation' (*ibid.*, p. 20, emphasis added). The level of participation may vary and the top of the ladder, whilst the ideal, will not be achievable for every student. This does not negate the importance of involving pupils at lower levels. It is crucial, however, to avoid tokenism and manipulation in place of genuine participation.

Community as a context

Citizenship cannot be viewed in a void, but needs to be seen within a context of people, relationships and within communities. Potter (2002: 7) suggests, 'Education for active citizenship is as much about feelings, a sense of belonging or of its opposite, alienation, isolation and anger. Above all citizenship education is about people.' This idea needs to be embedded within the ethos of a school, and within its classrooms and is especially important for those students at early stages of learning.

> At early key stages and for those at early stages of development (across the key stages), work within PSHE and Citizenship may help our pupils to develop their skills of responding to others, to help shape their understanding of the importance of communication and the value placed on these responses by others. It provides a real context in which we can support our pupils (especially at early stages) to learn about interacting with each other and the different means by which we each communicate. It offers opportunities beyond simple interaction, towards developing a caring 'community' in which we are each sensitive to the needs and preferences of each other; an environment in which we can ask for help or offer help to one another. (Fergusson 2001: 11)

Beyond the classroom and school is a wider context of people and communities. Claire's (2001) research in two inner-city primary schools emphasises the major influence of family and community on children's views and concerns. She comments that citizenship education must be set and evaluated within the wider context of children's lives, beyond the school. Thus 'the challenge for schools is not so much what to do within school, where the rules may be very clear and effectively enforced and where the children feel relatively safe; it is, rather, an issue of the "staying power" of the values of citizenship within the broader community' (p. 48). Claire's study involved children from largely working-class and ethnic minority backgrounds, whose family and community lives were lived by different values to those both implicit and explicit within the middle-class institution of school. It is interesting to relate this value differential between community and school to disability – the values promulgated within schools for students with learning difficulties through citizenship education of empowerment and advocacy may not be the public values of the wider community beyond school.

It is important for these reasons that we share an awareness and respect for our pupils' backgrounds in the same way we advocate they do of each other. To be able to do this a helpful approach is to start with a familiar focus for the pupil, an acknowledged valuable strategy for pupils with learning difficulties. By developing pupils' personal awareness, we have an opportunity to find out more about each individual ourselves as well as a chance to share this insight with their peers. From that base we are more effectively able to develop a true sense of community identity and belonging.

Hicks (2001) identifies four dimensions to citizenship which further support this idea:

- the personal dimension – this is 'the individual's search for integration and wholeness ... Thus building self-esteem, learning to work cooperatively, identifying one's personal stance on an issue and developing interpersonal skills are all essential prerequisites for developing a sense of oneself within society' (p. 12);
- the social dimension – this dimension 'recognises that our identity and sense of self only comes about through interaction with others' (p. 13);
- the spatial dimension – local, regional, national and global communities;
- the temporal dimension – set in wider context of past, present and future.

Intrinsic to the success of a 'community' is that it has a reciprocal relationship with its members, both being part of and belonging to each other. In this way, the school also needs to belong to the community it 'serves'. Pupils, parents and the local community should view it as 'our' school. As Cunningham (2000) points out, 'The school's own vision of itself is the essential foundation of any work in citizenship and participation' (p. 134). In order to achieve this with success, schools will need to involve those people in its 'life' in the same way as we are advocating pupil involvement.

The notion of community is explored in further detail in Chapter 4.

Inclusion

Schools then have a huge responsibility in the whole inclusion movement, not just within the life and work of the school, but also beyond school in the wider community. Citizenship education and all it entails – awareness, respect and involvement with and for each other, will enhance inclusion in its own right.

> The Citizenship curriculum incorporates explicit references to rights, diversity, mutual respect and understanding, fairness and social justice. The educators' task is to organise learning so that these values are apparent in the way material is taught as well as in the content of what is taught. *Perhaps Citizenship, more than any other subject, should start from a foundation of inclusion and equal opportunities practice.* (Jerome and Newman Turner 2001: 50, emphasis added)

Equally important, the impact of citizenship education will also promote an increase in the value placed upon inclusion and a greater insistence of its existence and progress.

The pupils themselves are at the heart of citizenship education. Therefore, we must start with the pupils. Others share this view, such as Claire (2001), who is adamant that citizenship is concerned with children finding their own voices, about children making their own agenda. This then is the challenge before us.

CHAPTER TWO

The citizenship curriculum

Introduction

This chapter describes the content of citizenship within the National Curriculum framework and programmes of study, and interprets and extends this for pupils with learning difficulties.

Citizenship is a complex curriculum subject. As the Association for Citizenship Teaching (2001) explains, it is a subject in its own right, a subject that can be delivered through other subjects and one which needs to be embedded in the life of the whole school.

PSHE and citizenship National Curriculum framework

Citizenship was included within the revised National Curriculum in 1999 (DfEE/QCA 1999a; DfEE/QCA 1999b). For Key Stages 1 and 2 it is integrated with Personal Social and Health Education and non-statutory guidelines are provided. For pupils at Key Stages 3 and 4 it became a statutory subject in September 2002. This is illustrated in Figure 2.1.

Key Stages 1 & 2	Key Stages 3 & 4
PSHE and Citizenship *non-statutory guidelines*	**PSHE** *non-statutory guidelines*
	Citizenship *statutory*

Figure 2.1 Citizenship in the National Curriculum

The PSHE and citizenship framework covers four strands:

- developing confidence and responsibility and making the most of their abilities;
- preparing to play an active role as citizens;
- developing a healthy, safer lifestyle; and
- developing good relationships and respecting the differences between people.

The second of these, 'preparing to play an active role as citizens', becomes the separate subject of Citizenship at Key Stages 3 and 4, while the remaining three strands are included within PSHE at these key stages.

The content of the PSHE and citizenship guidelines for Key Stages 1 and 2 and the programmes of study for Key Stages 3 and 4 are included within grids in the appendix of this book.

The programmes of study for citizenship at Key Stages 3 and 4 consist of three interrelated parts:

- **Knowledge and understanding about becoming an informed citizen.** This includes, for example, legal and human rights and responsibilities, the nature of government, the role of the media and global interdependence.
- **Developing skills of enquiry and communication.**
- **Developing skills of participation and responsible action.**

The framework also comprises a breadth of opportunities section for PSHE and citizenship (Figure 2.2). These opportunities are appropriate and relevant for *all* students, and some (for example encouraging and enabling students to make real choices and decisions) are frequently part of a school's overall aims.

- take and share responsibility
- feel positive about themselves
- take part in discussions
- participate
- make real choices and decisions
- meet and talk with people
- develop relationships through work and play
- consider social and moral dilemmas they come across in everyday life
- ask for help
- find information and advice; provide advice
- prepare for change

(compiled from all four key stages)

Figure 2.2 Breadth of opportunities through the National Curriculum PSHE and Citizenship framework

The Crick Report also identified three elements that run through all citizenship education:

Social and moral responsibility: Rights and responsibilities

'Pupils learning from the very beginning self-confidence and socially and morally responsible behaviour both in and beyond the classroom, both towards those in authority and towards each other' (QCA 1998: 11).

Community involvement: Communities and identities

'Pupils learning how to become helpfully involved in the life and concerns of their neighbourhoods and communities, including learning through community involvement and service' (QCA 1998: 12).

Political literacy: Democratic processes and government

'Pupils learning about the institutions, problems and practices of our democracy and how to make themselves effective in public life, locally, regionally and nationally through skills and values as well as knowledge' (QCA 2000b: 4).

Support publications

A range of publications is available from the Department for Education and Skills (DfES) and the Qualifications and Curriculum Authority (QCA) to directly support the implementation and delivery of the citizenship curriculum. These are summarised below in terms of their content and relevance for staff working with students with learning difficulties.

Citizenship guidance

PSHE and Citizenship at Key Stages 1 and 2: initial guidance for schools (QCA 2000a)

This explains the framework and suggests different ways of implementing it.

Citizenship at Key Stages 3 and 4: initial guidance for schools (QCA 2000b)

This booklet explains the importance of citizenship and discusses approaches to planning and implementing the citizenship programmes of study.

Planning, teaching and assessing the curriculum for pupils with learning difficulties: personal, social and health education and citizenship (QCA 2001c)

This is one booklet in a series of 15 providing curriculum guidance for staff working with pupils with learning difficulties. It includes ideas for interpreting and extending the different strands of PSHE and citizenship and for modifying the programmes of study. It also provides suggestions for key stage foci and activities, and P levels (performance descriptions leading up to level 1 of the National Curriculum) for assessment purposes. These were developed explicitly for staff working with pupils who may be described as having moderate learning difficulties (MLD), severe learning difficulties (SLD) or profound and multiple learning difficulties (PMLD) – pupils who are unlikely to achieve above National Curriculum level 2 at Key Stage 4.

Schemes of work

A scheme of work for Citizenship at Key Stages 1 and 2 (QCA 2002b)

A scheme of work for Citizenship at Key Stage 3 (QCA 2001e)

A scheme of work for Citizenship at Key Stage 4 (QCA 2002a)

These publications go further than previously published guidance and schemes of work for other subjects in terms of relevance and meaningfulness for pupils with learning difficulties. However, they are not specifically designed for these pupils and often require much adaptation.

Accompanying guidance for each scheme includes a teacher's guide and a booklet of ideas about pupil participation. Many units included in these schemes of work are relevant for students with learning difficulties:

Key Stages 1 and 2 unit titles:

- Taking part – developing skills of communication and participation
- Choices
- Animals and us
- People who help us – the police
- Living in a diverse world
- Developing our school grounds
- Children's rights – human rights
- How do rules and laws affect us?
- Respect for property
- Local democracy for young citizens
- In the media – what's the news?
- Moving on (year 6)

Key Stage 3 unit titles:

Discrete citizenship provision:

- Crime
- Human rights
- Britain – a diverse society
- How the law protects animals – a local-to-global study
- Government, elections and voting
- Local democracy
- Leisure and sport in the local community
- The significance of the media in society

Citizenship through other subjects:

- Citizenship and geography: debating a global issue
- Citizenship and history: Why is it so difficult to keep peace in the world today?
- Citizenship and history: Why did women and some men have to struggle for the vote in Britain? What is the point of voting today?
- Citizenship and RE: How do we deal with conflict?

Citizenship through wider curriculum activities:

- Developing skills of democratic participation
- Crime and safety awareness
- Celebrating human rights
- School linking
- Developing your school grounds

Key Stage 4 unit titles:

- Human rights
- Crime – young people and car crime
- Challenging racism and discrimination
- How and why are laws made?
- How the economy functions
- Business and enterprise
- Taking part – planning a community event
- Producing the news
- Consumer rights and responsibilities
- Rights and responsibilities in the world of work
- Europe – who decides?
- Global issues, local action

Further guidance

There are further guidance documents on specific aspects of citizenship and the relationship of citizenship to other subject areas:

- Careers Education in the new curriculum: its relationship to PSHE and citizenship at Key Stages 3 and 4 (DfEE 2000a);
- Developing a global dimension in the school curriculum (DfEE 2000b);
- Financial capability through personal finance education at KS1&2 (DfEE 2000c);
- Financial capability through personal finance education at KS3&4 (DfEE 2000d);
- First impressions: career-related learning in primary schools (DfES 2001a).

Citizenship for students aged 16–19

There are plans for citizenship programmes of study for 16–19-year-olds and a two-year pilot programme of projects is currently being undertaken managed by the Learning and Skills Development Agency (LSDA). The advisory group looking at citizenship for this age group (Further Education Funding Council 2000) made the following recommendations:

- Citizenship should be acknowledged as a Key Life Skill and should be given its proper place alongside the six Key Skills identified already.
- An entitlement to the development of citizenship – of which, participation should be a significant component – should be established which would apply to all students and trainees in the first phase of post-compulsory education and training.
- All such young adults should have effective opportunities to participate in activities relevant to the development of their citizenship skills, and to have their achievements recognised.

Citizenship and PSHE are clearly part of the 16–19 curriculum in preparation for adult life and (especially perhaps for students with learning difficulties) form a core part of curriculum entitlements and opportunities at 16–19.

Curricular implications for pupils with learning difficulties

When mapping the National Curriculum PSHE and Citizenship curriculum against that traditionally delivered to students with learning difficulties, there are many overlaps or familiar features. There are also aspects that are new and challenging. We have examined these in detail elsewhere (Lawson and Fergusson 2001). To summarise, however, many of these new and more challenging elements were in the area of citizenship, for example: democracy, government and law; social, political, cultural and moral issues; participation, negotiation and decision-making; interdependence; and environmental sustainability. There were also aspects of the traditional PSHE curriculum that do not fit easily with this differing National Curriculum framework, for example: personal care skills; daily living skills; and play, leisure and recreation skills. Many of these elements can now be appropriately addressed by following the guidance materials for Developing Skills (QCA 2001b).

The importance of PSHE and citizenship for pupils with learning difficulties is outlined in the QCA guidance materials for pupils with learning difficulties (QCA 2001c):

> Learning PSHE and citizenship help all pupils develop as individuals in a wider society. Pupils learn to understand themselves physically, emotionally, socially and sexually and to understand their relationships with others.

> In particular, PSHE and citizenship offers pupils with learning difficulties opportunities to:

> - make choices and decisions
> - develop personal autonomy by having a degree of responsibility and control over their lives
> - make a difference or make changes by their individual or collective actions
> - find out that there are different viewpoints which lead to a respect for the opinion of others.

> (QCA 2001c: 4)

This concept of importance is very similar to that for typically developing pupils. The booklet also develops the meaning of citizenship education for pupils with learning difficulties, particularly for those at the earliest levels of development:

> Knowledge and understanding of citizenship starts by pupils interacting with adults they know and other pupils in familiar one-to-one activities and small group situations, as well as taking part in the regular routines, roles and responsibilities of classroom and school life. Pupils learn about the right and wrong ways to behave through the boundaries set by others. Citizenship gives contexts in which all pupils, particularly those with learning difficulties, can move from a personal view of themselves and their immediate world, towards a much wider perspective. This helps them think about other people and ways in which they can make a difference to others and the world around them. Pupils learn about the differences in people and how to value those differences.

Teaching this aspect across the Key Stages can help pupils to:

- make choices
- take part in group activities and discussions
- realise that all individuals are important in their own right
- recognise differences and similarities in people.

> (QCA 2001c: 5)

Considering the three elements of citizenship noted in Chapter 1 – rights and responsibilities, communities and identity and government and democracy – for pupils with learning difficulties is, at first glance, challenging. However, when examining these more deeply, the first two are to some extent at least implicit in much of our practice with pupils with learning difficulties. The latter, the political literacy component, appears more daunting and, we would suggest, relates to some of the aspects of power discussed in Chapter 1 in that it is reliant upon staff ensuring pupils have a voice and can be effective in their lives.

Flexibility and inclusion

A number of statements within the QCA guidance indicate the flexibility of the PSHE and citizenship framework:

> The framework for PSHE and citizenship is designed to be 'light touch' and flexible, so that schools can build on what they are already doing well and develop a curriculum that is relevant to their children, connecting with their interests and experiences, and relating to their abilities and backgrounds. It should also provide children with opportunities to address real-life issues and show them that they can make a difference. (QCA 2002b, Teacher's guide: 3)

Thus, adaptation, interpretation, exemplification and innovation are entirely appropriate and actively encouraged. It is also emphasised that individuals and groups of pupils will experience citizenship in different ways.

Inclusion

The statutory inclusion statement in the National Curriculum – *Inclusion: Providing effective learning opportunities for all pupils* (DfEE/QCA 1999a: 30–7) – gives flexibility in the modification of all programmes of study. Each of the teachers' guides accompanying the QCA schemes of work has a section entitled 'inclusion', which indicates further flexibility of approach, based on this inclusion statement, in order to take account of the 'different experiences, strengths and interests of their pupils':

Teachers should consider whether:

- particular parts of the scheme should be emphasised or expanded;
- pupils should be given more time for particular aspects of the scheme or given opportunities to progress more rapidly;
- particular pupils need opportunities to revisit knowledge and skills in different contexts;
- to use these materials as a resource for developing an alternative scheme. The alternative must offer pupils opportunities to experience a range of work across key aspects drawn from the programme of study.

If adapting particular units, teachers should consider whether:

- the expectations and learning objectives need modifying;
- there is a need to add challenge by increasing the demand;
- there is a need to provide small steps, short, guided and more focused tasks and supporting structures to enable pupils working below the demands of learning objectives to undertake the activity;
- the outcomes need to be changed to take account of revisions to the objectives and activities, or because pupils will operate on different levels;

- to vary contexts, resources, or teaching and learning styles to take account of the different learning needs of boys and girls, and the needs of pupils from different social and cultural backgrounds and with different lifestyles; and
- the activities need to be adapted to provide support for pupils with difficulties in communication, language or literacy.

(QCA 2001e, Teacher's guide: 19)

The inclusion statement also suggests the possibilities of choosing material from earlier key stages; and the maintaining and consolidating of current work, as well as tackling new knowledge, skills and understanding.

This position gives schools flexibility to develop approaches to meet the changing needs and interests of its students and school community. In doing this, a school will have more ownership if its own particular aims, ethos and values come first. When Citizenship and PSHE are truly embedded in the life and work of a school then they develop a reciprocal relationship with its **ethos and values**; they each permeate, influence and enhance the other – a two-way process.

PSHE and citizenship encompass: knowledge and understanding; skills; and attitudes and values.

Knowledge and understanding

Knowledge and understanding can be extended for pupils with learning difficulties to include 'awareness', in addition to 'knowing' and 'understanding'. Thus, for example, pupils may:

- be aware of familiar people;
- know their likes and dislikes;
- understand the concept of growing from young to old.

The knowledge and understanding aspect of citizenship within the National Curriculum can be divided into the three interrelated elements (as outlined on pp. 12–13) of:

- social and moral responsibility – rights and responsibilities;
- community involvement – communities and identity; and
- political literacy – government and democracy.

The QCA schemes of work provide a useful framework, relating to each of these three elements, and exemplify questions which are framed from the pupils' perspective. Examples from these are shown in Figures 2.3, 2.4 and 2.5. This is an interesting stance as it approaches citizenship from the pupil's point of view. Such questions are pertinent for **all** pupils, though interpretation, context and teaching and implications will vary. We have also used these three elements as the main headings of Chapter 5 to group ideas and suggestions for citizenship activities.

Social and moral responsibility: rights and responsibilities

'Rights and responsibilities' (Figure 2.3) is concerned, for example, with human and legal rights rules, laws, fairness, making choices, bullying, the police and the legal system. It is also about conflict resolution; people having different tastes, preferences and views; recognising and coping with emotions and feelings; resolving differences and compromising.

Rights and responsibilities

Key Stages 1 and 2	Why do we need rules and laws?	What pressures and influences affect me?	Crime and punishment
	• What are my basic needs and the needs of others? • What do I think is fair or unfair? • What are human rights? • Why do we need rules and laws? • How are our class and school rules made?	• What affects the way I make decisions? • What influences my choices? • What is peer influence and how can it affect me? • What influences my spending? • How do the media portray social issues?	• What is crime? • What do I know about crime in my community? • How does our local police force help us? • Why do people commit crimes? • What happens if someone breaks the law?
Key Stage 3	Why have rules?	Young people and the law	Crime and punishment
	• What are my rights and responsibilities at home and at school? • What rules apply in my school and how are they decided? • What protects my rights and how can I access that protection? • What causes conflict and how do I resolve it?	• Why do I think people commit crimes? • Why does society need laws? • What would happen to me if I broke the law? • How does the Human Rights Act affect me?	• Why should lawbreakers be punished? • What do I think are fair and unfair punishments? • Who decides on punishments and by what criteria? • How do prisons and other institutions work?
Key Stage 4	Why have rules?	The law	Crime and punishment
	• How are my rights and responsibilities changing? • What do human rights have to do with me?	• How does the law protect me as a consumer? • How are the rights and responsibilities of employers and employees protected?	• What happens to victims and offenders? • What is the role of the courts in making and shaping law?

Figure 2.3 Rights and responsibilities: questions framed for pupils (drawn from: QCA 2002b: 31; QCA 2001e: 25; QCA 2002a: 23)

Communities and identity

	Me and my school community	Me and my wider communities	National and global citizenship
Key Stages 1 and 2			
	• How are we the same and different? • Why do our communities change? • How can we prepare for change? • How can we help people new to our community? • What is bullying and how do I deal with it?	• What is my local community like? • Who can help us in our local community? • How do I understand sameness and difference in my own and other communities? • What is racism and how do I respond to it? • What are the rights of children?	• What are other communities like? • What are places and people like in other parts of the world? • How are we all connected? • How can I investigate national and global issues? • How can I contribute to a sustainable future?
Key Stage 3	Me and my local community	National identities	Global citizenship
	• What are my identities? • What groups/ communities do I belong to and how can I contribute to them? • What do I think about my local community? • What is the diversity and difference in my community and how is it celebrated?	• How can different communities learn from each other? • How do I understand diversity and how is it represented locally, nationally and globally? • How tolerant am I of diversity and difference? • What are the legal and human rights and responsibilities that underpin society?	• Is there a global community? • What organisations have a global role, accountability and significance? • How do voluntary groups contribute to local and global development and understanding?
Key Stage 4	Me and my local community	National identities	Global citizenship
	• How do/could I use my skills in my community? • How can I work with others to build partnerships in the community?	• How does the media represent national, regional, religious and ethnic diversity?	• What links do I have with Commonwealth and other international communities? • How can I participate in global issues?

Figure 2.4 Communities and identity: questions framed for pupils (drawn from: QCA 2002b: 31; QCA 2001e: 25; QCA 2002a: 23)

Government and democracy

Key Stages 1 and 2	Communicating and taking part	Democracy at school and locally	Learning about democracy and government
	• How good am I at speaking and listening to others? • How do I communicate my views to others? • How do I contribute to discussion? • What do I contribute when I work with others? • How can I help others at school?	• What kind of decisions do I make? • How do we make informed choices? • How can my decisions affect others? • How do I contribute to decision-making in my class and school?	• Who represents you, me, us? • How are local facilities funded? • What does a local councillor do? • What does my MP do? • How can I have a voice?
Key Stage 3	Democracy at school and locally	Learning about voting and government	Government in the wider world
	• Where in my life do I contribute to decision-making? • What do I understand about fairness in decision-making? • Who represents my interests and how can I influence them – in school and in local government? • What do I understand by the term 'democracy'?	• How are laws decided and made? • What are the roles of local and national government? • How can I have a voice? • When and how do I vote and what is the point of voting? • What is an election and how can I participate in one?	• What do I know about the EU, Commonwealth and United Nations? • What different systems of government are there in other parts of the world? • Why is it difficult to keep peace in the world?
Key Stage 4	Democracy at school and locally	Learning about voting and government	Government in the wider world
	• How do I communicate and represent the interests of others? • How do I contribute to group and team work?	• What do I know about how parliament makes and shapes the law?	• How does the EU affect me? • How do different governments react to and influence global issues?

Figure 2.5 Government and democracy: questions framed for pupils (drawn from: QCA 2002b: 31; QCA 2001e: 25; QCA 2002a: 23)

Community involvement: communities and identity

This element (Figure 2.4) includes local community links, voluntary groups, community facilities, charities, fundraising and links with other communities. It comprises diversity and identity, different groups, religious and ethnic identities, differences between people, stereotyping and racism. Furthermore, it encompasses global and environmental issues, allocation of resources, recycling and interdependence.

Political literacy: government and democracy

'Government and democracy' (Figure 2.5) is concerned with: responsibility and power within and beyond school, participation, making views known, systems of government; with voting and elections, making decisions, expressing views, debate, ways of collecting opinion and differences of opinion. It covers the role of the media: fact versus fiction, advertising, the news media and the effect of media. In addition it encompasses public services and the economy.

Jerome and Newman Turner (2001) present some suggested 'entry level' and 'basic level' objectives for Key Stage 3 citizenship based on the themes contained within these three elements. They also identify what aspects of the Key Stage 1 and 2 non-statutory guidelines could be included within each theme, thus making links across key stages. These precise learning objectives and the cross-key stage connections are particularly useful for pupils with learning difficulties.

Skills

Skills are 'can do' actions, responses and behaviours. They may include making choices, giving permission and taking turns at early levels of development.

ACCAC (2000), the Qualification, Curriculum and Assessment Authority for Wales, divides skills for PSHE (which includes citizenship in their curriculum documentation) into:

- communication skills
- inter-personal skills
- intra-personal skills
- problem-solving and decision-making skills
- study skills
- practical skills.

These skills are likely to need explicit teaching.

Skills are an integral part of the programmes of study at Key Stages 3 and 4 as the knowledge and understanding strand is developed through skills of enquiry and communication and skills of participation and responsible action.

Skills of enquiry and communication

This includes thinking about topical issues, problems and events, analysing information and sources, expressing and justifying opinions and contributing to discussion and debate. What does this mean for pupils with learning difficulties? How will they access these aspects?

As previously stated in Chapter 1, it is useful to analyse this from two angles – on the one hand, extending back the content and, on the other hand, considering what thinking about topical issues, or expressing an opinion or contributing to debate might mean for pupils with learning difficulties.

Key questions in thinking about topical issues are centred around the Who? What? Where? When? Why? In order to express and justify opinions, pupils may perhaps first be helped to shape and develop a point of view; they may indicate what they feel about something, thus expressing their view. To contribute to discussions and debates pupils may first learn about some necessary ground rules, such as listening and respecting the view of others, or they may work on the development of communication skills or the use of other strategies (e.g. alternative and augmentative communication modes such as a symbol board) to express their own viewpoint. Teaching and learning approaches including discussion and debate are explored in Chapter 4.

Skills of participation and responsible action

This includes how to consider the experiences of others, take part responsibly in activities and reflect on the process of participation.

This stems from working with others, working in teams and taking on different roles within a team. It may include circle time, school council experiences and a range of class, school or community projects. Participation was examined as a concept in Chapter 1 and is further investigated in Chapter 4.

Attitudes and values

Attitudes and values are about thinking and belief, and seem, at first, hard to unpack for pupils with learning difficulties. However, if you consider what some of these attitudes and values might be, or actually look like in practice, it is easier to relate to; for example, self-respect, respect for others, responsibility, willingness to cooperate and sensitivity to the environment.

Oxfam (1997) considers the area of global citizenship in terms of knowledge, skills, and attitudes and values. Examples from this, shown in Figure 2.6, are clearly relevant for pupils with learning difficulties.

This review of the citizenship curriculum and requirements will, hopefully, enable practitioners to identify with many features that already hold a profile within their current practice. The following chapter seeks to place citizenship within the whole curriculum framework.

Knowledge and understanding

Social justice and equity	Diversity	Globalisation and interdependence	Sustainable development	Peace and conflict
• What is fair/unfair • What is right and wrong • Awareness of rich and poor • Fairness between groups • Causes and effects of inequality	• Awareness of others in relation to self • Awareness of similarities and differences between people • Contribution of different cultures, values and beliefs to our society • Nature of prejudice and way to combat it	• Sense of immediate and local environment • Awareness of different places • Sense of the wider world • Links and connections between different places • Trade between countries • Fair trade	• Living things and their needs • How to take care of things • A sense of the future • Our impact on the environment • Awareness of the past and future • Relationship between people and the environment • Awareness of finite resources • Our potential to change things	• Our actions have consequences • Conflicts past and present in our society and others • Causes of conflict and conflict resolution – personal level • Causes of conflict • Impact of conflict strategies for tackling conflict and for conflict prevention

Skills

Critical thinking	Ability to argue effectively	Ability to challenge injustice and inequalities	Respect for people and things	Cooperation and conflict resolution
• Listening to others • Asking questions • Looking at different viewpoints • Developing an enquiring mind • Detecting bias, opinion and stereotypes • Assessing different viewpoints	• Expressing a view • Beginning to state an opinion based on evidence • Finding and selecting evidence • Beginning to present a reasoned case	• Beginning to identify unfairness and take appropriate action • Recognising and starting to challenge unfairness	• Starting to take care of things – animate and inanimate • Starting to think of others • Empathising and responding to the needs of others • Making links between our lives and the lives of others • Making choices and recognising the consequences of choices	• Cooperating • Sharing • Starting to look at resolving arguments peacefully • Starting to participate • Tact and diplomacy • Involving/including society and others • Accepting and acting on group decisions • Compromising

Values and attitudes

Sense of identity and self-esteem	Empathy and sense of common humanity	Commitment to social justice and equity	Valuing and respecting diversity	Concern for the environment and commitment to sustainable development	Belief that people can make a difference
• Sense of identity and self-worth • Awareness of and pride in identity • Sense of importance of individual worth	• Concern for others in immediate circle • Interest and concern for others in wider sphere • Empathy towards others locally and globally	• Sense of fair play • Sense of personal indignation • Willingness to speak up for others • Growing interest in world events • Sense of justice	• Positive attitude towards difference and diversity • Valuing others as equal and different • Willingness to learn from the experiences of others • Growing respect for difference and diversity	• Appreciation of own environment and living things • Sense of wonder and curiosity • Concern for the wider environment • Beginning to value resources • Willingness to care for the environment • Sense of responsibility for the environment and the use of resources	• Willingness to admit and learn from mistakes • Awareness that our actions have consequences • Willingness to cooperate and participate • Belief that things can be better and that individuals can make a difference

Figure 2.6 Knowledge and understanding, skill, attitudes and values for global citizenship (adapted from Oxfam 1997)

CHAPTER THREE

Citizenship in the whole curriculum

Introduction

This chapter examines the position of Citizenship within the whole curriculum and explores approaches for organising, auditing, planning and assessing citizenship.

Citizenship has implications for the whole school – for management and organisation as well as both the explicit and implicit curricula, for governors, the whole staff and pupils.

Approaches to the organisation of the citizenship curriculum

Strategic planning will identify opportunities for Citizenship through the processes of auditing and monitoring. Flexible approaches to the organisation of Citizenship will offer access and meaningful contexts, in addition to a realistic means of coverage. Examples of these in different settings are given later. Whole-school developments may also provide alternative or additional contexts for Citizenship activities; for example, through initiatives such as the government's healthy schools standards, or the Eco-schools award (www.eco-schools.org.uk).

The National Healthy School Standard Scheme (DfEE 1999c, 1999d) provides a context for identifying and developing shared values within a school and its community. It offers a framework through which schools, staff, pupils, parents and local community members can work together on projects which will be of mutual benefit to the school and beyond. It creates opportunities for individuals and groups (pupils, parents, culturally diverse groups) to have a voice, to be involved in or have representation in decision-making about 'making a difference'.

It includes themes of:

- local priorities
- school priorities
- PSHE
- citizenship
- drugs, alcohol and tobacco
- emotional health and well-being (including bullying)
- healthy eating
- physical activity
- safety
- sex and relationships education.

The criteria for assessing the Citizenship component of the Healthy School Standard are:

- the school recognises that all aspects of school life can have an impact on the development of pupils in becoming informed, active and responsible citizens;

- the school provides opportunities for pupils to be actively involved in the life of their school and communities. (DfEE 1999d: 15)

The very process of this initiative is inclusive from the outset, with an expectation for schools to involve pupils, staff, parents and the local community at each level of decision-making and development. This inclusive approach is seen as an integral aspect to the success of a school in being accredited with the Healthy School Standard. The initiative provides 'real-life' opportunities to develop understanding, awareness and mutual respect for people and the environment where they live, learn and work together. Once these values are embedded within the school and community, then true inclusion, both educational and social, is a greater possibility, at least at a local level.

Other approaches for citizenship delivery may be via, for example,

- discrete curriculum time;

- other subjects/curriculum areas/cross-curricular topics or modules;

- regular routines;

- whole-school ethos;

- class culture;

- extension activities and school events; and

- involvement in the life of the school and community, e.g. school councils/ playground buddy.

Citizenship takes place in different contexts and involves a range of experiences for pupils. The contexts and experiences might include circle time, a visit to a council chamber, working in a small group, the school council, meeting visitors from the local community, a fundraising activity or a theatre group. Such a range of approaches to delivery is actively encouraged by the DfES and QCA publications.

Discrete curriculum time

It may be necessary, or even more appropriate, for some aspects of Citizenship to be addressed as discrete sessions – some aspects of political literacy or topical news issues, for example. These timetabled sessions might be led by 'visitors' or those with particular experience, expertise or training – for example, a councillor who is involved in forthcoming local elections. This approach to delivery is less likely in early key stages.

Advantages	Disadvantages
<ul><li>easily identifiable; easy to plan for</li><li>separate subject identity</li><li>aids progression</li><li>makes assessment and reporting easier</li></ul>	<ul><li>risk of repeating content from other subjects</li><li>may marginalise subject, e.g. only taught by subject specialists</li><li>timetable demands</li><li>may discourage whole-school approach</li></ul>

Other subjects/curriculum areas/cross-curricular topics or modules

Planned opportunities for citizenship can be provided in other subjects. Some aspects appear to fit more naturally with specific subjects, for example religious beliefs and values in RE, moral stories in English and cultural diversity in music. There are also clear links with careers education and work-related learning (DfEE 2000a) and Grimwade *et al.* (2000) indicate how geography and citizenship education are closely linked.

Integrating citizenship with PSHE has clear advantages in terms of linking with a complementary subject and initiatives, e.g. the Healthy School scheme. It is appropriate across the age range and key stages. However, by not recognising citizenship as a distinct area of learning, it may be marginalised and there are aspects of it which may be best approached discretely, particularly at later key stages.

There are *some* key elements of the subject which should occur in all subjects – for example, opportunities to make choices or decisions, involvement in discussions, learning about fairness and or working with others.

> Teaching and learning in all subjects can offer opportunities for promoting the school's ethos and developing children's confidence and sense of responsibility, by giving children the chance to: show what they are good at and what they like; share their opinions; learn new skills; make the most of their abilities; develop relationships; respect the difference between people; recognise how their behaviour affects others; listen and work cooperatively, and reflect on their learning. (DfEE 2000: 13)

Coverage may be addressed through cross-curricular approaches: at early key stages – for example in projects based on themes such as 'People who help us'; later through topics or modules focused on, for example, 'current affairs' or 'investigating the local community' or 'accessible leisure facilities'; or via a thematic approach when examining rules and laws.

Advantages	Disadvantages
• all staff involved; whole-school approach • aspects of Citizenship will be developed where most applicable • enriches other subjects	• if in a subject-based department/school, not everyone may feel confident about teaching Citizenship • difficult to create awareness of Citizenship as a distinct and important area of learning • potential difficulty of gathering enough evidence to support assessment and reporting • danger of tokenism

Regular routines

These familiar and regular routines, for example break times, circle time or assemblies, offer real-life opportunities to learn and practise skills of choice-making, turn-taking, listening to and respecting others, among many others. In addition, they provide an invaluable way of integrating citizenship into everyday (school) life. However, it is not sufficient to just be aware that this happens; it also needs to be consciously identified and planned for.

Advantages	Disadvantages
• 'real' opportunities for choice-making • familiar contexts • expectations clear • opportunities to develop independence	• pupils respond as they feel they are expected to/used to • no generalising opportunities

Whole-school ethos and class culture

The culture and ethos of a school will play an interactive role in Citizenship education. To some extent, a role model is presented to students through the ethos of the school, the teaching approaches and attitudes adopted by the staff, the relationships between staff and pupils and the dignity and respect afforded to the pupils. This aspect of addressing Citizenship needs to be examined by staff, in order to give it the high profile it should demand. Potter (2002: 265) highlights this perspective as essential: 'the culture of the school is central, not incidental, to citizenship education.'

All aspects of school need to be recognised as 'playing a part' and, therefore, need to be acknowledged. It is not enough to say 'we are doing it all the time', without consciously having some intentions as to what, why and how we are 'doing it all the time'. Are we including, most importantly, *all* the people involved in school – for example lunchtime staff, transport escorts and parents? Do we keep them all informed of the purpose and strategies by which we can act consistently?

Citizenship is reflected in the ethos of the school. In practice this includes, for example, the school mission statement, clearly stated citizenship aims, the general atmosphere of the school, and consulting and valuing all members of the school. Klein (2001), drawing on the work of the Development Education Association, suggests the following create a school's ethos:

• underpinning values – trust; honesty; equality; justice.
• student participation – school councils; clubs; extra-curricular; community activities.
• learning environment – physical; emotional.
• relationships – pupil–pupil; pupil–adult; adult–adult; management.
• policies and standards – mission statements; citizenship policies; equal opportunities; anti-bullying behaviour; playground policy.
• participation of whole school community (regular visitors)

You may have further items to add to this list.

Potter (2002: 266–7) suggests the following questions in analysing whole school ethos:

• Are people welcoming, confident and helpful?
• How do students and staff relate to one another?
• What is the general feel of the place? Is it relaxed, calm and purposeful, or confused and tense?
• Where is the discipline coming from, from within or without?
• How participative are the students as learners, as citizens and as members of a local community?

As Rowe states,

> Learning what it means to be an active and participating citizen is not confined to lesson time; it goes on throughout a child's whole school life. We need to be aware of the messages children pick up from everything they experience in school. (Rowe 2001: 41).

It is therefore important, he suggests, to identify precisely which citizenship experiences have an impact on citizenship learning. Where and how in the school do pupils learn about fairness, power, conflict, cooperation? What does it actually mean when we state that we respect pupils? Where do pupils experience democracy in action?

Some schools have worked on such questions to develop a staff charter, reflecting on the aims and values of the school in practice, in concrete and tangible ways. Figure 3.1 shows an example of this from Watling View School.

Advantages	Disadvantages
• adults and others provide role models • students can anticipate how others should behave or respond • individuals and their opinions or choices are valued • school is a supportive learning environment	• students may expect everyone to act as they do at school • the 'real world' is not as predictable • individuals are not always respected outside school • learning away from school may be the 'hard way' • difficult to ensure coverage and progression

Extension activities and school events

Some aspects of Citizenship cannot easily be addressed through any of the approaches mentioned so far. It may be necessary to create opportunities for additional activities to meet these unmet areas. For example, residential experiences, special/theme days, charity fundraising, theatre-in-education, artists-in-residence, mini-enterprise schemes and public performances may provide essential opportunities and realistic contexts. Special events or visits by outside speakers, visits to local amenities or to see people in their roles at work may also offer valuable insights for students in making their learning more meaningful.

By extending the range of contexts in which students learn about or practise what they have learnt, we enable them to be more active participants in life beyond school and into adulthood.

Advantages	Disadvantages
• fun and different for students • encourages broad range of activities • realistic learning opportunities • opportunities to work with new people	• does not integrate throughout year • may miss important topical events • potential difficulties with assessment and reporting • may not be easily replicated for future learning/students

To ensure that pupils are as prepared as possible for all the opportunities, experiences and responsibilities that are available as they progress through the school and into their adult lives

We make sure that we use age-appropriate language, behaviour and resources with our pupils so they are presented with good models for themselves.

We pitch our lessons so that each pupil is stretched and challenged to achieve.

We revisit key areas of learning and experience as pupils progress through the school so they become confident in their understanding.

We encourage our pupils to keep trying so they can enjoy a sense of achievement when they succeed.

We allow our pupils to make mistakes in a supportive environment so they learn how to deal with them in the future.

We help our pupils to learn about taking responsibility, both for their own behaviour and when carrying out tasks.

We give our pupils the skills to handle increasingly difficult situations.

We help our pupils face their worries and find ways to overcome them.

We teach our pupils how to carry out routine hygiene tasks with increasing independence.

We teach our pupils domestic skills so they can play a useful role in family life.

We teach our pupils everyday life skills which will help them to be as independent as possible, for example using a bus or the telephone.

We offer our pupils many opportunities to socialise in the local and wider community so they can learn to adapt to new situations.

We teach our pupils how to behave towards other people both in school and in the community.

We help our pupils to understand that they have rights and we give them the confidence to speak for themselves whenever possible.

We teach our pupils that they have choices and that sometimes it is alright to say 'No'.

We encourage our pupils to evaluate their own work and to be involved in setting new targets for themselves whenever appropriate.

We offer our older pupils placements on college and work training/experience schemes so they can learn real-life responsibilities.

We offer older pupils appropriate career guidance.

We help older pupils to prepare for post-school placements, whether in work, college or new residential accommodation.

We encourage pupils to experience a variety of leisure interests as a preparation for life outside school.

Figure 3.1 Waiting View School: Aims in Action

Involvement in the life of the school

'Citizenship education is also about democracy in action. Students and pupils have a significant part to play through participating in the life of the school' (Potter 2002: 101). It is easy to agree with this statement, but in reality how well do we uphold this principle? We are quick to identify aspects of curriculum or access we feel to be tokenistic, but is this also an area where we too often pay 'lip service' to a very important part of the student learning process?

We readily acknowledge that this participation is perhaps the greatest opportunity of all to take part in real decision-making that affects their own lives and learning in school. However, what mechanisms exist for all pupils to contribute their views? Most schools have developed an inclusive approach to involving students in their own annual reviews, but what about the wider aspects of school life that impact directly upon them – in curriculum planning, for example? Other aspects to explore may include representation and involvement in:

- governors meetings;
- policy reviews;
- the school development plan;
- school publications;
- running the school – welcoming, showing visitors, answering the telephone, leading assemblies, collecting and giving information;
- the school council; and
- peer support.

Advantages	Disadvantages
• focus on action • learning applied and real • encourages/motivates students • students can identify with the part they have played in 'making a difference'	• difficulties in meaningful access • others valuing their abilities or contributions • finding time for this part of the process within the school day

Involvement in the life of the community

'Citizenship education also requires pupils to learn through taking positive action in their local and wider communities' (Potter 2002: 102).

Advantages	Disadvantages
• focus on action • learning applied and real • develops links with community groups • easier to generalise outside of school (community)	• difficult to organise • difficult to use for all aspects of the curriculum

Incidental/spontaneous opportunities

Misperceptions of restricted time availability and a too-prescriptive curriculum may be cramping the previously creative nature and talents of school staff. It is all too easy to lament the passing of pre-National Curriculum teaching which offered flexibility to 'abandon' planning in response to incidental or spontaneous events that occur in school life. We can redress the balance by consciously acknowledging the value in these 'real life' opportunities as often the most meaningful contexts for learning; by each having an understanding of the knowledge, skills or understanding of citizenship and PSHE that may be addressed within these situations. Fergusson (2002) cites the example of discovering the class tomatoes have died due to lack of watering, leading to a discussion about responsibilities, or a break-time incident leading to a discussion about fairness and respecting others' views.

Some may argue, as discussed earlier with reference to whole-school ethos, that we are 'doing citizenship' all of the time, and to some extent that is true. However, these occasions, events, opportunities need to be explicitly and consciously recognised and planned for in order to 'exploit the potential' for citizenship education. Lees and Plant (2000) suggest a list of questions to ask when identifying opportunities in order to confirm their potential. They were working in the area of personal and social development – the questions apply equally to citizenship and we have adapted them to that purpose below.

When identifying the opportunities the following questions need to be addressed:

- What particular kinds of opportunity does the subject/activity offer to promote citizenship?
- Are all pupils involved in the activity?
- Does planning for the subject/activity include citizenship?
- Are pupils encouraged to reflect on what they have learned about themselves and their relationship with others?
- In relation to citizenship, how does the subject/activity focus on what pupils: are able to do (skills); know and understand (knowledge); and have thought about (attitudes and values)?
- Does the subject/activity offer the opportunity to teach, practise or assess citizenship skills?

(adapted from Lees and Plant 2000: 20)

Mapping and auditing

An audit is a good starting point; it will probably reveal that many elements of citizenship are already covered, within schemes of work for other subjects, in daily routines and in the context of cross-curricular or wider curricular activities. There is a danger in assuming that citizenship is only a matter of labelling however. An audit will also reveal gaps in provision.

Jerome and Newman Turner (2001: 8) outline the uses and importance of auditing:

- it gets a wider group of people involved and informed
- it can help to identify strengths and weaknesses
- it can build confidence by showing that you are not starting from scratch
- it should help you to avoid unnecessary duplication
- it provides a sound starting point for planning.

The Association for Citizenship Teaching (2001) provide basic audit questions:

- What does the school already provide in terms of knowledge, understanding, skills, and concepts? How does this match with the programmes of study and non-statutory guidelines?
- Where is citizenship being done in the school?
- Are the entitlements of pupils and their communities being met?

They provide the example of examining the concept of 'democracy':

- How does this apply to the life of the school?
- Where in the life of school are the pupils experiencing democracy in action?
- In the school/class council?
- In the conduct of the school?
- In the conduct of parents' evenings?
- In shaping class/school values statements?
- In helping shape the school environment?

Rowe (2001) similarly provides a list of questions to consider when developing a whole-school approach to citizenship. He groups these according to curriculum, ethos, policy and community involvement. For example:

Curriculum

- Does the school curriculum provide sufficient opportunity for the development of knowledge and understanding at the same time as developing skills of enquiry and communication and participation?
- Are all members of staff aware of the range of resources which can be used for citizenship work? (e.g. is there a list of recommended story books for different ages which focus on citizenship themes?)

Ethos

Is an attitude of respect and partnership extended to the children and all those involved in caring for them?

Policy

- Does the overall policy framework for the school take account of the fact that education for citizenship is seen as a fundamental aim of education, as set out in the Statement of Values for curriculum 2000?
- Does the school do all it can to ensure equality of access to learning for all its pupils?

Community involvement

- Are there opportunities in the community to enhance the children's citizenship learning?
- Does the curriculum provide opportunities to invite visitors from the community to talk about their work? Are the visits well prepared for? Are the children involved in setting the agenda and making visitors welcome?

From Rowe 2001: 42–3

In order to make the audit information to be of most value, you can tailor the questions further, ensuring they reflect the needs of your school population and are specific to your context. For example, What does citizenship mean for this group of students? What is the priority for this Key Stage? What is the priority for this pupil?

There are a number of ways of auditing and mapping using grids. Jerome and Newman Turner (2001) provide a number of different photocopiable auditing sheets for secondary schools embracing curriculum coverage, staff needs and students' perceptions. Abbott (2000) offers examples and blank grids for mapping statements in the non-statutory guidelines for PSHE and Citizenship at Key Stages 1 and 2 to different modes of delivery (e.g. extension activities, cross-curricular, whole-school).

Some examples

Staff at Lakeside School studied the PSHE and citizenship framework in the revised National Curriculum and adapted and interpreted the knowledge, skills and understanding for their pupils with severe and profound and multiple learning difficulties. The 'preparing to play an active role as citizens' strand for Key Stage 1 is reproduced in Figure 3.2.

Preparing to play an active role as citizens

Pupils should be taught:

a) to share news, and take part in simple reviews of what they may do as a class

b) to recognise the choices they can make and recognise the difference between right and wrong

c) to recognise, name and deal with their feelings in a positive way

d) to comply with the routines, procedures and rules of the class, with explanations to reinforce understanding

e) to realise that people and other living things have needs, and they have responsibilities to meet them

f) to realise that they are part of various groups and communities, e.g. home/school

g) that some things harm the environment, e.g. throwing litter, damaging trees, drawing on walls

h) to contribute to school life, e.g. going on 'errands', taking part in assemblies and celebrations

i) to realise money has a purpose and can be used for different purposes, e.g. class shopping, tuck shop

---

Figure 3.2 Lakeside School: Adapting the knowledge, skills and understanding, Key Stage 1

After making modifications, the school was then able to map where this altered interpretation fitted within the overall picture. They prepared an audit which looked at provision, how and when it was delivered, and identified possible changes and additions. Early development of careers education was also identified – marked by a ©. Figure 3.3 illustrates this for the citizenship strand for Key Stage 1. They also identified activities which accessed the breadth of opportunities (Figure 3.4).

Content	Changes and additions	Current provision	When delivered	How delivered and resources	Examples of activities
Preparing to play an active role as citizens Pupils should be taught:					
a) To take part in discussions with one other and class ©		Turn-taking – allowing others to speak, listening and responding, eye contact, good body language	Cross-curricular and English	Group sessions and 1:1 on speech and language work	Registration and news, drinks time, discuss play activity with one other or a group
b) To take part in simple debate about topical issues ©		Involving children in informing them and asking opinion on day to day activities within classroom – infants in school	Beginning of day or session relate to everyday activities	Group work – use of symbols, objects of reference, pictures	Give children opportunity to actively get ready for sessions, e.g. gather ideas for swimming or big book literacy
c) To recognise choices they can make and difference between right and wrong ©		Children begin to be aware of the group in that their choices may not always be available at that time. They may have to wait, correct procedure, right and wrong.	Cross-curricular	Individual work in group context. Use symbols to reinforce concepts.	Use pictures of situations. Children encouraged to identify good/bad. Use puppets to demonstrate right and wrong. Role play where appropriate.
d) To agree and follow rules for group and class, understand how rules help them ©	Discuss school rules with children – infants using symbols – and why we have them	Children aware of rules of classroom and school. Reinforced verbally.	Cross-curricular assembly	Group work and 1:1. School rules in symbols. Class rules displayed.	Reinforce through praise – keeping to school rules
e) To realise people and living things have needs, they have responsibilities to meet them		Children may have to wait whilst others in group have needs met. Children encouraged to care for others' welfare in group, e.g. carrying a cup, picking up a dropped toy for people in wheelchairs. Looking after living things, fish, plants.	Cross-curricular	Students given opportunities to support peers	Caring for others, giving out drinks, picking up toys for students in wheelchairs. Looking after plants – watering. Plant a planter and care for it.
f) What improves and harms local, natural and built environments; some of the ways people look after them ©	Infants could clear up the playground or woodland. Plant bulbs and flowers	Nursery – tidy classroom – safety	Cross-curricular and work on Environment, Science/Geography	Group work caring for environment – internal and external	Cleaning classroom, looking after bathroom, e.g. turn off taps and lights. Litter collection in playground.
g) To contribute to life of class and school ©		Nursery – become responsible for class task Class tasks – register, collection of cups	Cross-curricular	Encourage individuals through praise and reward for their contributions	Class jobs, collecting hymnbooks in assembly, stacking chairs, carrying tissues or equipment, putting away equipment
h) To realise money comes from different sources and is used for different purposes ©		Know that money comes from home. Can identify things that need money (tuck shop, shopping, paying for drinks)	Maths, tuck shop and visits to community	Group work and 1:1 – real-life, practical activities	Get together money for tuck shop, pay in shop for items bought, discuss bill when out for drinks

Figure 3.3 Lakeside School: Audit of current provision, Key Stage 1

PSHE, CITIZENSHIP AND CEG	
Content	**Activities to access opportunities**
All pupils need to be given opportunities to:	
Take and share responsibility	Begin to have responsibility for our belongings, hanging up coats, carrying bag, tidying and putting away equipment
Feel positive about themselves	End-of-day assembly, students sharing their successes with others in class, positive feedback for good work, behaviour or effort
Take part in discussions	Use of age-appropriate resources as discussion points on global differences
Make real choices	On eating, choosing toys to play with, drinks
Meet and talk with people	Children given opportunity to meet and interact with people in school and visitors
Develop relationships through work and play	Children given opportunities to work with other children, choose who to play and work with and learn about sharing
Consider social and moral behaviour dilemmas that they come across in everyday life	Children are taught about right/wrong within the context of the group
Ask for help	Children know who to ask for assistance through sign, eye pointing, speech, gesture

Figure 3.4 Lakeside School: Activities to access the breadth of opportunities, Key Stage 1

Sunfield School involved all staff at an INSET day, to identify where aspects of Citizenship were being covered for each Key Stage. Part of this audit for Key Stage 4 is shown in Figure 3.5.

Moving on

An audit needs to be comprehensive and not complacent. Once completed, the data need examination – what gaps are there? In what depth do we cover that element? How can we make this more accessible or challenging? Ofsted (2002), reporting on preparations for the introduction of citizenship in secondary schools, suggest that the best audits have a 'qualitative dimension', particularly recognising 'the key difference

Knowledge and understanding about becoming informed citizens

	Discrete curriculum time	Cross-curricular, through other NC subjects	Whole-school ethos	Class cultures	Extra-curricular and community links
b) Diversity and identity The origins and implications of the diverse national, regional, religious and ethnic identities in the United Kingdom and the need for mutual respect and understanding	Circle time PSHE Religious Festivals RE Food technology	RE Geography Music Art Morning words English – photo album and family book PSHE	Assembly Prayers Religious Festivals/ celebrations Golden Rules Mission Statement Uniforms	Appropriate behaviour towards peers Where we live – map in class/house ASDAN – international relations, increase understanding of other countries and religions Individual Education and Care Plans	Church Places of worship Where we live – map in class/house ASDAN – international relations, increase understanding of other countries and religions Cheers and reward board
c) Government The work of parliament, the government and the courts in making and shaping the law	History PSHE Geography Accreditation modules	Literacy Cookery Symbol use/ English Transition planning	Choices Student Council Elections	Choices Visit by local MP Day trip to Houses of Parliament ASDAN – rights and responsibilities Use of choice time to indicate wants – for sensory room, etc. Use of symbol system Involvement in class management Individual Education and Care Plans	Day trip to Houses of Parliament Regular contact with MP ASDAN – rights and responsibilities Social and Educational visits Café visits

Figure 3.5 Sunfield School: Part of Citizenship audit Key Stage 4

between work that is implicit and thus supportive of citizenship, and work that is explicit, which is the core of citizenship teaching and learning.'

Potter (2002: 143) warns that, whilst necessary, 'audit sheets can easily foster the tick-box mentality in which we lose the big idea behind citizenship education ... though useful for making a quick review of what is happening, [it] tends to encourage convergent thinking'. Thus it may serve to reinforce past practices rather than challenge and open new possibilities. We need also to ask then, what else can we do that is new and innovative? How can we address the more difficult aspects or offer more challenging opportunities?

A citizenship policy

> A policy which is clear about how Citizenship fits in with the wider objectives of the school will be helpful to visitors and new staff. It will also help to clarify accountability and ensure that citizenship is monitored and evaluated effectively. An initiative which is so wide ranging may be easier to understand once it has been translated into specific action points and responsibilities. (Jerome and Newman Turner 2001: 11)

Jerome and Newman Turner (2001) recommend the following framework of headings for a school policy on citizenship:

• Overall aims
• Process of developing the policy
• Responsibility
• Curriculum issues
• Learning knowledge
• Learning skills
• Assessment and reporting
• Equality of access and inclusion
• Ethos
• Student involvement in decision-making
• Feeder schools
• Parent
• Local community
• Evaluation
• Confidentiality
• Controversial issues
• Links with other policies and initiatives
• Other issues

The DfES citizenship website (www.dfes.gov.uk/citizenship) also contains ideas for a policy framework:

• An introduction, including rationale and aim, and the principles
• How sensitive moral, social and political issues are to be addressed
• Teaching and learning approaches
• Staffing
• The involvement of visitors and external groups
• The role of pupils in participation and responsible action
• The commitment to community involvement and the implications for child protection

- An outline of the resources that are to be made available
- Level of in-service training and support that is required
- Monitoring and evaluating
- Policy review date.

School policies need to encompass all staff and pupils in a school, including the teaching assistants, lunchtime supervisors, administrative staff, caretaker, kitchen staff and transport escorts.

Organisation and planning

We have, in this chapter, discussed in full a range of approaches to citizenship organisation. Jack Taylor School has decided to approach citizenship in a cross-curricular way for Key Stages 3, 4 and post-16 provision, with specific lessons being incorporated at Key Stage 4.

Citizenship lessons are integrated into the PSHE curriculum. Different aspects of the citizenship curriculum are covered via other subject areas as shown in Figure 3.6. At Key Stage 4 students receive one term of specific citizenship lessons.

This demonstrates just one approach, that suited the practice of that school, but flexibility is firmly advocated. QCA guidance (QCA 2000b), for example, outlines three approaches to citizenship, which can be used in combination:

- a concepts or themes approach, providing broad headings, e.g. sustainable development; human rights, cooperation and conflict; individual and community;
- a skills approach, based on skills of enquiry and communication (for example, studying media coverage, carrying out surveys, interviews) and skills of participation and responsible action; and
- an enquiry approach – investigating aspects through questioning What? Why? How? When? Where?

Whichever route is chosen, certain considerations may keep us on track. When planning the curriculum, Lees and Plant (2000) suggest that a scheme of work should answer the questions Who? What? When? Where? and How?

Figure 3.7 shows a term's scheme of work on rules, laws and keeping safe for a group of students with learning difficulties in years 10 and 11 at Montacute School.

Emily Fortey School encompasses Citizenship within its PSHE curriculum. It is a skills curriculum and a knowledge curriculum. The knowledge curriculum is explained and the Citizenship part of it shown in Figure 3.8.

An example of their scheme of work is illustrated in Figure 3.9. As explained in Figure 3.8, this represents one academic year.

Assessment in citizenship education

Requirements for assessment, recording and reporting

Key Stages 1 and 2

There is no statutory requirement for end-of-key stage assessment for these key stages. As for all subject areas, 'Schools are required to keep records for every child, including information on academic achievements, other skills and abilities and progress made in school' (QCA 2002c: 3) and 'schools must report to parents brief comments on the child's progress in each subject and activity studied' (*ibid.*) This means where PSHE and Citizenship are included in the curriculum, they should be reported upon – either with a brief commentary on progress or as part of other activities in the school curriculum.

Citizenship Curriculum Map

Key Stages 3 and 4

The following aspects are covered within all curriculum areas:

Roles and responsibilities
Mutual respect
Dealing with conflict
Democratic participation/communication

Specific links are listed below and are delivered as part of the term's topic in each subject area:

PSHE
Public and community services
Behaviour
Human rights and conflicts
Health
Safety

Science
Human rights
Animal rights
Hazards and risks
Topical studies

Geography
Developing areas
Communities

Religion
Diversity of religions/identities
Celebrations/festivals

Work-related Learning
Developing areas
Communities and business

History
Global issues
Peace and conflict

Drama
Justice systems
Debate and contribution

English
Media
Debate and contribution

MFL
Global issues

Music
Diversity of identity
Media

CDT
Hazards and risks

PE
Leisure and sport

ICT
Global issues
Media

Maths
Diversity of identity
Topical issues

Art
Global issues

The following areas within the secondary/post-16 department all contribute towards an holistic approach towards the delivery of citizenship:

Accreditation system
School journeys
The common room
School link with other mainstream schools
The school shop
School celebrations
College links

Figure 3.6 Jack Taylor School: Citizenship curriculum map, Key Stages 3 and 4

SCHEME OF WORK – CITIZENSHIP/GLOBAL AWARENESS

Dates: Autumn Term 2001   Times: Weds 1.40–2.40pm

Group: Senior 3

Staff:

AIMS: To begin to develop an understanding beyond the pupil's own experiences and build up some knowledge of his/her future role in society. To keep safe.

LEARNING OBJECTIVES/ASSESSMENT OPPORTUNITIES

For all pupils:

- To understand why we need to have rules and Laws.
- To acquire some knowledge and understanding of the Democratic Process.
- To know what happens if Laws are broken.
- To know how we can keep ourselves safe on the roads and at home.
- To make sensible choices, saying 'Yes' or 'No'. Practise assertiveness.
- On completion, pupils will have participated in discussions, elections, role-play activities, made decisions, visited 'Streetwise', a Magistrates Court, Poole Council Chambers and talked to the Community Policeman.

ACTIVITIES (see lesson notes)

- RULES AND WHY WE NEED THEM:
  Class/School Rules: If we make the rules it is up to us to see they are not broken. All except X are members of the School Council. Make class rules and affirmations.
- LOCAL AND NATIONAL DEMOCRACY:
  Use Internet to find out information about Parliament, Political Parties, Voting Rights.
- WHAT HAPPENS IF PEOPLE BREAK LAWS:
  Community Policeman, Magistrates Court, High Courts, Judge, Jury, Defendant, Prosecute, Witness, Guilty, Innocent, Oath, TV programmes, role-play, visit from magistrates. How we can be good citizens.
- KEEPING OURSELVES SAFE:
  Visit 'Streetwise', a safety interactive centre in Poole.
  'Stranger-Danger' – LDA Protection Pack, Video, Role-Play, P.52. YES/NO Skills, asking and giving permission, voicing opinions, listening to others, developing an awareness and understanding of 'strangers' in all kinds of settings. X and Y will need special guidance – use of PEC's.
- SAFETY IN SCHOOL, AT HOME, ROAD SAFETY, WATER SAFETY, SAFETY AT PLAY:
  Gardens, community, home protection, neighbourhood watch, road signs, motoring laws, road safety, lifeguards, safety signs in swimming pools and on the beach, telephone skills, emergency services, role-play.
- RESOURCES:
  Reference Books, *A curriculum for PSHE, Healthworks* resource material, videos, LDA Protection Pack, road safety material, bright safe clothing, newpaper, court hearings (see lesson notes). Visits will be made to 'Streetwise', Magistrates Court, the Civic Centre, Council Chamber. Visit from Community Policeman.
- CURRICULUM REFERENCES NC PSHE Citizenship
- CURRICULUM LINKS: English, Maths, ICT, History, PSHE, RE
- ACCESS: Minibus for visits.
- EVALUATION: End-of-lesson notes (see Teacher File).
  Module Assessed for ASDAN. Transitional Challenge.
- RECORDING: Pupil Citizenship folders. Digital and video camera.
- PROGRESSION: Reinforce and expand on knowledge and understanding when in post-16 Group.

Figure 3.7 Montacute School: One term's scheme of work for citizenship

Emily Fortey School

Personal, Social and Health Education Knowledge Curriculum

Our knowledge curriculum for Personal Social and Health Education is divided into three Programmes of Study (Ourselves, Relationships and Citizenship), each containing eight Schemes of Work.

Each Scheme of Work represents one academic year, and is divided into three terms.

As well as introducing new knowledge and concepts, we regard these Schemes of Work as opportunities for pupils to develop, practise and extend the PSHE they are learning from the skills curriculum.

Citizenship

Community links

- Public amenities and services
- Different roles of people in society – people who help us
- Recognising and naming familiar amenities and features of the community
- Rules, regulations and the law in the community
- Right and wrong in society – police, courts, consequences
- How do we get our news?
- The media and how it affects our opinions

Careers education and the world of work

- Different jobs and careers
- Work experience
- Influencing our future

Care for environment

- Care of other people's property and respect for immediate environment
- Making your property safe
- Creating a pleasant environment – 'cared for' and 'uncared for'
- The wider community and world environment

Community projects

- Voting or taking group decisions
- Doing things for others, e.g. sponsored events
- Identifying waste and rubbish

Figure 3.8 Emily Fortey School: PSHE knowledge curriculum and Citizenship component

	Ourselves	Relationships	Citizenship
Scheme 7 Term 1:1	**Avoiding exploitation (2)...** Which parts of our bodies are private/public. Which self care routines are private. (What is a private place and a public place.) *(See Sex Education Policy: 'Avoiding exploitation' and 'Gender Concepts and Growing up')*	**Different types of families (2)...** Marriage and different types of relationships. Friends and family/living with friends. The value of family life (however it is made up). *(See Sex Education Policy: 'Adulthood')*	
Scheme 7 Term 1:2	**Staying safe (3)...** Revision module on: Safety in the home/school Road safety Stranger danger		**Public amenities and services...** Using a mobile phone Buses Libraries Leisure centres Cinemas, etc.
Scheme 7 Term 2:1		**Bullying, racism and discrimination...** Their effects and how to challenge them	**Doing things for others...** Sponsored events; or Consideration for the world environment
Scheme 7 Term 2:2	**Medicines and drugs...** When is it safe? Situations to avoid. When to say 'yes', when to say 'no'. *(See Drugs Education Policy)*	**Reproduction and contraception (1)...** *(See Sex Education Policy: Reproduction and Contraception)*	
Scheme 7 Term 3:1	**Seeking help if unsure or in difficulty...** Emergency and procedures: In school At home In the community Using a telephone to seek help		**Right and wrong in society...** Police, courts, consequences. Speaking up against crime or dishonesty.
Scheme 7 Term 3:2		**Facing new challenges and life changes positively...** What might happen to you over the next few years? Who to talk to about it?	**School elections or voting** Taking group decisions. Accepting the decision. Democracy at work.

Figure 3.9 Emily Fortey School: PSHE knowledge curriculum – Scheme 7

43

Key Stage 3

There is a statutory requirement to assess pupils' attainment in citizenship at the end of Key Stage 3 from summer 2004, and there is an end-of-Key Stage 3 description provided in the National Curriculum (DfEE/QCA 1999a). 'The summary assessment should be based on knowledge of how the pupil achieves over time across a range of contexts, taking account of pupils' strengths and areas for development' (QCA 2002c: 4). Schools must keep a record of pupils' progress and achievement. This may include a record of whether pupils are working towards, achieving or working beyond the key stage description. Schools must report to parents on pupil progress in citizenship during Key Stage 3.

Key Stage 4

There is no statutory requirement for end-of-Key Stage 4 assessment in citizenship. The advice is that schools should choose the most appropriate methods of assessing progress and recognising achievement. 'A range of awards, certificates, portfolios and qualifications can be used to recognise attainment in citizenship...' (QCA 2002c: 6).

There is an end-of-Key Stage 4 description provided in the National Curriculum (DfEE/QCA 1999a). Schools must report to parents on pupil progress in citizenship during Key Stage 4.

Principles of assessment in Citizenship

Underlying principles of assessment are particularly important in citizenship. As citizenship emphasises active learning and active participation it is essential that pupils are actively involved in assessment processes too (see Lawson 1998). This can be through self- and peer assessment and through the collection and selection of appropriate evidence. Ord (2002) suggests that the method of assessment can be a citizenship objective in itself. 'Established methods of evaluation, such as journals, project work, video and before/after assessments and so on can obviously contribute, but other more innovative approaches should be introduced.'

Thinking about the purpose of assessment is also particularly pertinent in citizenship. Assessment in citizenship is concerned with the development of skills and participation as well as knowledge, but is not about the assessment of values and attitudes. It is not about judging the value of an individual – you cannot fail as a citizen! It is crucial to return to the adage that 'we should assess what we value rather than value what we assess'. As Campbell (2000: 4) notes:

> In citizenship it is particularly *important* that assessment methods provide ways of recognising the achievements of **all** pupils... The challenge is to find ways of measuring what we value in citizenship education, including the vital participative element, rather than valuing only those aspects that are easy to measure.

It is thus also important to consider progress in a multidimensional way, as suggested by QCA general guidelines for pupils with learning difficulties (QCA 2001a). In particular, for PSHE and citizenship, it is recognised that pupils may make progress by:

- moving from contact with others in class and school to community involvement;
- developing greater control and choice;
- adapting to change as they grow and develop, physically and emotionally;

- moving from the personal to a wider perspective (in terms of the range of relationships and viewpoints, and consideration of other people's point of view);
- moving from an immediate time perspective to thinking about the future and reflecting on the past – for example, how tackling things differently could lead to different outcomes.

(QCA 2001c: 4)

Ideas for assessment

The QCA (2002c) *Citizenship at Key Stages 1–4: Guidance on Assessment, Recording and Reporting* includes examples of how different schools may organise their assessment, recording and reporting in relation to their citizenship provision. For example, at one school, for Key Stages 1 and 2:

> *Citizenship provision*: specific citizenship activities within weekly PSHE and citizenship lessons; regular circle-time activities; citizenship also linked with literacy and combined with humanities.
>
> *Recording progress*: each child has a passport of citizenship achievement, in which they collect stamps and stickers for specific, identified achievements. At the end of each year, they choose the achievement of which they are most proud and record it in the class citizenship book. The year 6 book is further developed into a leavers' book, a copy of which is presented to each child.
>
> *Reporting to parents*: children write a short statement about their achievement for inclusion with the class teacher's comments in the annual report to parents.
>
> (QCA 2002c: 11)

In another school, a special school for pupils aged 3 to 19:

> *Citizenship provision*: citizenship is central to the whole curriculum – many other curriculum areas are delivered through citizenship. Special events involve parents and the wider community.
>
> *Recording progress*: included in pupils' individual education plans; citizenship objectives are recorded by their class teacher; pupils add personal statements to the individual records. Stickers and certificates recognise particular achievements throughout the school. Some pupils in Key Stage 4 gain entry-level qualifications in citizenship.
>
> *Reporting to parents*: addressed at annual review meetings; teacher and pupil statements are included in annual reports.
>
> (QCA 2002c: 12)

Assessment could be linked to precise objectives. The 'basic level' and 'entry level' objectives identified by Jerome and Newman Turner (2001) may be useful in this context. For example, within the theme 'Diversity and identity' the following objectives are included:

> - Identify self as member of different groups
>
> - Recognise others as member of different groups
>
> - Experience/appreciate examples of activities/sensations/flavours/stories/sounds/music, etc. of different cultures
>
> (Jerome and Newman Turner 2001: 58)

Staff and pupils may, of course, prefer to set their own personal objectives in Citizenship.

The QCA guidance material for pupils with learning difficulties contains P levels (pre-National Curriculum levels from P1 to P8) for all subjects, including PSHE and citizenship (QCA 2001c). These are based on a 'framework for attainment' (QCA 2001a) from 'Encounter', through 'Awareness', 'Attention and response', 'Engagement', 'Participation' and 'Involvement' to the 'Gaining of skills, knowledge and understanding'. They may provide a useful tool for summative assessment where staff decide which description best fits a pupil's performance over a period of time and in different contexts.

It is important to emphasise **assessment *for* learning**, in addition to the assessment *of* learning. This is especially so in the context of citizenship because it is more than skills, knowledge and understanding; it is also about participation and involvement. Assessment methods which encourage ongoing assessment, personal involvement in assessment and reflection on learning and participation need to be developed. Records of achievement or progress files, for example, may provide an ideal format for this type of assessment. The use of citizenship portfolios would extend this opportunity further.

Accreditation

There are some accredited awards for citizenship, including entry level awards. Many schools, for example, use the ASDAN (Award Scheme Development and Accreditation Network, see useful websites) accreditation schemes for pupils at Key Stage 4 and post-16 – for example, Transition Challenge, Towards Independence and Youth Award Schemes. These all have substantial elements of PSHE and Citizenship. ASDAN also accredit citizenship skills and activities through their *Life Skills* series. At entry level 1, for example, there is a section on 'decision-making'. The following are requirements with supporting evidence:

Activity 1

Identify decisions that you make in your daily life.

Identify three things that you decide for yourself.

Activity 2

Show you can contribute towards a group decision.

Identify one occasion when you took part on a group decision. Include the following details:

- what you were deciding;

- who you were deciding with (e.g. friends, family, peer, others);
- the choice of at least one other member of the group;
- your choice;
- how the decision was made (vote or agreement);
- what was decided.

(ASDAN, Life Skills, Entry 1, Unit E1 Citizenship, Section 3: Decision-Making)

There are also other ways of both internally and externally accrediting achievement – for example, school certificates, community awards, Duke of Edinburgh Awards.

Self- and peer assessment

Self assessment can be as straightforward as responding with a smile to convey 'like' or choosing a happy or sad face symbol to represent a pupil's contribution to a particular activity or as complex as identifying the areas of the programme of study in which they have made progress over the last term. (Institute for Citizenship 2002: 16)

In citizenship especially, students' views should be considered. Jerome and Newman Turner (2001) include some examples of self- and peer assessment which are appropriate for some pupils with learning difficulties. For example, students could use peer assessment to look at the roles played within a group, asking each other 'Did I listen to other people's views?' Students could use yes/no faces, symbols, or thumbs up/down to respond.

In reviewing participation, students could consider:

What have I participated in?

What did I do as part of the activity?

What skills did I use?

What was I happy with?

What was I good at?

What did I have difficulty with?

What would I do differently next time?

Photographs, objects, symbolic and pictorial lists, for example, can be used to encourage participation in this reflection and evaluation.

This chapter has given an overview of the place of citizenship within the whole curriculum. Identifying the flexibility and the opportunities to plan for delivering the subject is just one element necessary to addressing citizenship; the very nature of this area demands also that we scrutinise and reflect on our practice and teaching approaches. This wide-ranging theme is examined in the next chapter.

CHAPTER FOUR

Citizenship: Teaching and learning approaches

Introduction

In this chapter, different approaches for teaching and learning in citizenship are explored and developed for pupils with learning difficulties. There are strong overlaps between this chapter and the more specific activities identified in Chapters 5 and 6.

Those who have worked in the citizenship field for some time advocate principles that already hold a high profile within the world of severe and profound and multiple learning difficulties. It is because we view this as such a new subject to address that it is easy to forget what we know to be good practice, so it is important that we 'return to first principles'. If we think about citizenship and PSHE in this way, it is about how we work with these pupils, the process of their learning, that is so crucial.

We would also suggest that for much (but not all) of the coverage, it is valuable to view and address PSHE and citizenship together. In this way, they support and provide a valuable context for each other. For example, by starting with personal, self-awareness as a starting point or foundation, it is easier to then look to create opportunities to move beyond this, to develop a greater awareness and understanding of the wider world.

Community, Pedagogy and Participation, we would suggest, are essential aspects demanding a refocus when considering the implications of our teaching and learning approaches. These aspects make up, and are set within, the ethos and values of our schools.

Community

In itself, the notion of community can be difficult within many school settings, but particularly in special settings where students travel outside of their neighbourhood to school and come from a range of geographical areas. In addition, they will each have individual and diverse backgrounds. It is important, therefore, that we start with a personal perspective, particularly for those at the earliest levels. In so doing we may need to interpret the idea of community as beginning with the individual. For example:

- **self** – awareness, personal interests and preferences, control of the personal environment, personal identity, expanding personal experiences to understand these are my feelings and responses;
- **self and others** – to be aware that others can respond in different ways, have preferences and interests that are different from mine. Begin with familiar 'others', then actively move on to introducing 'new' others (for example, working with other adults, group work or with peer support);
- **mini communities** – my class, specific activity or interest groups I belong to (horse-riding group or Panjabi literacy group), moving on to groups that are different from normal collaborative work models, within the classroom (swimming club, school council).

When we employ such 'first principles' (starting from a familiar focus and building on it), we can move on to the more traditional interpretations of 'community':

- **class/whole school/local community/national and global** – learning about, and through being a part of, these wider community groups.

For some pupils the concrete everyday environs of the classroom provide their community. However, such a continuum is not intended to imply inaccessibility or lack of entitlement to learning opportunities and the establishment of relationships within the local community or, indeed, the global world.

This overview of 'community' fits well with the dimensions outlined by Hicks (2001, see also Chapter 1). Four dimensions to citizenship were identified as the personal, the social, the spatial and the temporal. These dimensions reflect the very personal perspective as a starting point before moving out to the wider world viewpoint.

We need also to bear in mind that *community* has an added dimension and importance. It is also about the ethos of *being* a community, of *belonging* to the school, the classroom, the drama group. It is the very belonging, valuing and respecting of everybody that is important and a responsibility of each of us. That is to say, it is about, in essence, *developing inclusive practice*. It is the very essence of inclusion.

Sapon-Shevin (1999) identifies the following characteristics in defining a sense of community within a classroom:

- security – it is safe to be yourself, it is possible to take risks, it is alright to ask for help;
- open communication – individual differences and difficulties are openly acknowledged;
- mutual liking – pupils and staff are encouraged to know and like and support each other;
- shared goals and objectives – the class work **with** each other, challenges are set for the class as a whole;
- connectedness and trust – being part of a whole.

She suggests that students need to feel safe and nurtured in order to be both empowered and engaged. Staff needs are the same.

Barriers to the establishment of such a community, Sapon-Shevin indicates, are:

- **exclusion**, as a response to diversity, through the fearing of differences; and
- **competition**, where the focus is on success rather than learning. In a competitive environment differences can be a liability (she envisages musical chairs) and pupils may be discouraged from taking risks.

Pedagogy

We must be concerned with the extent to which pupils and students are encouraged and enabled to become active participants in teaching and learning.

Active learning

The principles of active learning underpin citizenship – the importance of involving students in the learning process through interactive, participatory methods of teaching.

Rowe (2001: 14) maintains, 'The learning of citizenship values takes place through **thinking, feeling and doing**.' However, for many of our pupils, their experience of life will have been very different from that of their mainstream peers. That is, for a variety of reasons associated with their learning or other disabilities, their experiences and opportunities will have been severely restricted or their interpretations of events will not necessarily have been meaningful. How then can we compensate for this in our work with these pupils?

This dilemma is by no means new to us. It is the challenge we face across the curriculum and beyond. What is new is this 'take' on developing beyond PSHE; building on the focus of personal development, to learn how we as individuals affect others in the world. We each have 'a part to play', and the responsibility for taking part as best we can is the new perspective.

We have identified aspects of citizenship which present a real challenge, some are either abstract in their concept or beyond the experience of many pupils. Some concepts will be about experiences we hope pupils never encounter – for example, keeping themselves safe from abuse. For many such ideas, we will need to create, often artificially, a means of conveying some understanding of situations in which certain ways of acting can have differing consequences (again, the example of personal safety) in order to prepare pupils as best we can for a wide range of 'real life' events.

Meaningful contexts

It is essential to create opportunities that are *real*. Within the field of learning difficulties, we already know the importance of this for our student group. It becomes more necessary, in particular, when we try to meet the challenges of some of the more abstract concepts within citizenship. This is where there are overlaps between what Kerr (2000) describes in terms as education *about*, *through* and *for* citizenship. It may be *through* a context where students learn about how different people behave that they can learn *about* what is right or wrong, in order to understand how to be responsible citizens.

Returning to first principles – the role of 'others'

We know from child development theories and the psychology supporting these that much learning is dependent on the role of others to interpret, shape and give meaning to actions and their consequences. Our experience of supporting youngsters with learning difficulties further strengthens this role of 'others', as being crucial to learning becoming meaningful and functional. For those at the earliest levels, this is confirmed further.

Relationships

We need to examine the roles and status of relationships, to ensure there is maximum equity between staff and pupils: to look at the 'power base' within relationships and its flexibility and movement; to allow opportunities for the lead role to be a moveable one, where adults may at times follow the lead of students. For students at the earliest levels, this may be the first stage in their realisation that they can have an effect on their life, their world and others in it.

Developing staff–student relationships that empower students to take an active part in their learning process involves two-way trust and respect to allow risk-taking (albeit in a safe form). To experience mistakes and consequences of actions in themselves offers meaning to learning. To employ this flexibility and approach is not an easy task by any means – it challenges our practice and the notion of 'teaching'. It is essential, however, if we are to give and practise the message that we value our students and their offerings, in whatever mode they are presented.

This approach within the context of active learning is summarised by McLaughlin and Byers (2001: 72):

> The current notion of active citizenship builds on the active learning approach. The learning needs to be based in the world of the student and it involves action. If students are to learn from their own experience and to struggle with what that means then teachers will have to allow a certain amount of risk. Letting students be responsible for their own learning means that teachers have to allow students to struggle. It also means giving real responsibility to the students so that they can really struggle.

Interaction and engagement with others

We have discussed some elements of the 'role of others' and the crucial part they play. The interactive approaches that we adopt form a very significant factor in enabling our students, particularly those at the earliest levels. This is where our professional expertise becomes more than just 'teaching'.

The development of interactive approaches in special schools was firmly established before the introduction of the National Curriculum. Along with other aspects of the good practice that was current at that time, the profile of such an interactive way of working diminished, as practitioners strived to meet the new curriculum demands. Most of the focus within schools was on subjects, content and planning for coverage. It was some time later that schools revisited teaching and learning approaches, but this time within the subject context.

When examining practice from the established citizenship education field, there is much that parallels our philosophies and our best practice. But, as previously alluded to, schools are again in a position of viewing citizenship as 'another new subject' with the focus currently firmly set on content and coverage issues rather than on the most effective and appropriate means of delivery. There is a necessity for us to 'return to first principles', to re-examine the approaches that we know to be crucial in enabling our students to develop. The whole of PSHE and citizenship is about interaction with and about others, and as Potter (2002: 173) states, 'The distinguishing mark of active learning...is *interaction* and engagement with other people.' It is a vital facet of addressing citizenship education that we actively include this element in our work.

The role played by 'others' is more than one of just support or teaching; we need to act as interveners, facilitators or enablers. It is the way in which others respond to the student or interpret their behaviours that shape and consolidate meaning and development. We can transfer what we know to be of good practice for those functioning at the earliest or pre-intentional levels of communication and development; to recognise it also to be 'best practice within the area of PSHE and citizenship'. For example, it is by consistent responding of parents and staff, that students learn to have some control in their life – to begin to realise that their actions can have an effect.

Once those routines are established we have the next challenge – to enable them to learn to be able to anticipate, and then to progress to being able to actively participate, and then on to initiating intentionally. In the same way, we know that we, at the earliest stages, have learnt about 'right and wrong', for example, by the way others react, or not, to our behaviour.

What is demanded is an evaluation of our working in this way at a 'whole school' level. We need to:

- re-visit interactive approaches – to enable students and create those meaningful opportunities we have identified;
- consciously plan and facilitate involvement of peers – by demonstration or by giving responsibility to students;
- share the status and use of all modes of communication – to demonstrate that speech is not the only mode used consistently;
- truly develop consistent responding by all involved – not just classroom staff; and
- actively seek to widen interactive networks – by expanding the repertoire of 'familiar' relationships you expand the notion of community and, therefore, also widen opportunities.

These approaches will involve sharing and training throughout the school community (and beyond the classroom) of students as well as adults. There is a need for individuals to be able to recognise and be able to sign, use symbol boards, look for eye movements or increased finger activity, for example, as valid modes of communicating and participating.

Another factor we need to consider is that of individual or preferred learning styles of pupils. How do they as individuals learn best? What is the approach or mode of learning that they are most responsive to? Some pupils prefer to learn visually, for example, and will respond well to photographic information (e.g. photo scenarios or facial expressions); others may need the whole multisensory, 'all-singing, all-dancing' approach. For this reason, we will need to provide numerous and differing opportunities, contexts and approaches to ensure our teaching is most meaningful to every pupil. In addition, we need to build in opportunities for our students to demonstrate their learning and their understanding of it.

Peer interaction

The concept of interaction between peers is given great importance within the field of learning difficulties. It is, however, an ideal we perpetually strive to achieve, with many of our students being socially excluded or isolated from their peers (at school or their home neighbourhood). For a whole host of reasons, it is not an 'easy option' for our student groups – there are communication difficulties or communication that is not of a standard form; early levels of development where the purpose or intention to communicate has not been established; or where an individual's behaviour is a barrier to interactional experiences. These examples tend to be the norm rather than the exception in many school settings. In our planning we continue to provide opportunities for collaboration between students, often with limited success or where the interaction never goes beyond the planned context. There may be a case, then, for giving a focus to this goal outside of other educational activities. That is to specifically plan situations and support that enable positive 'social connections' to be established.

Much work addressing this issue has been developed in the adult learning disabilities field, through 'Circles of Support' networks, and usually alongside Person Centred Planning approaches, where the individual becomes the sole focus of planning. A Circle of Support is a group of people, directed by a facilitator, which helps individuals to achieve their personal goals in life. The 'circle' acts as a 'natural support network' and the *'focus person* is in control of who to invite into the circle and where to direct the circle's energy' (Otorepec 2002). A description of this approach in a school setting by Otorepec offers some insight of how to structure a personalised circle time for one student. The activity demonstrates the positive 'values of inclusion in practice through inclusive play and games'. Otorepec's case study outlines how a short time – regularly at the end of lunch breaks – was identified as a time to develop meaningful friendships for one young woman with challenging behaviour. The peers who joined Sarah's circle were encouraged to talk positively about Sarah and make their own observations as a way of increasing their understanding of Sarah and how important friendships and interaction are to everybody. This study highlights benefits to all who are involved and not only to the *focus person* – a chance to learn from each other. It sees this as an opportunity to 'embrace diversity', focus on strengths and concentrate on empowerment where personal choices are valued. 'Building and strengthening community links . . . increasing the chances of . . . friendships' in addition to 'overcoming social exclusion and making a positive difference to the quality of . . . life' (p. 32).

Participation

We have addressed the importance of active learning earlier in this chapter. This notion can be further explored now by raising the issue of participation by students. It is crucial that we avoid tokenism and manipulation in place of genuine participation.

Levels of participation

Hart (1992, cited in Holden and Clough 1998), as described in Chapter 1, suggests a 'ladder of participation' that describes levels of participation. For students with learning difficulties, however, as we noted, this may not be a totally inclusive model as it stands, as it suggests certain prerequisites or levels of development as necessary to truly participate. A more flexible interpretation may be required.

We are offered guidance in the QCA *Planning Teaching and Assessing the Curriculum for Pupils with Learning Difficulties* materials (QCA 2001a) about progression through levels of involvement. This framework was developed from established practice within the fields of severe and profound and multiple learning difficulties (Brown 1996) and multisensory impairment (McInnes and Treffrey 1982), and offers a more inclusive progression.

Giving people a voice

Developing autonomy in our students is a huge challenge. As part of this development of supporting we may need to begin as advocates on their behalf. By the very nature of their early levels of learning and communication, many of them do not make demands. We need to create a voice for them or provide opportunities in which they can express themselves to some degree, however small.

Sense of agency

As part of true participation, we need to engender a sense of agency among our students. To achieve this we need to foster real roles in achieving change, in making a difference. Having an identified role in any project or process is so important, providing it has a real purpose. To experience being part of a process where everyone has a real part to play, however small, but where each is seen to be of equal value, is imperative. It is the whole picture that we each add to; for example, by enacting the story of 'The Enormous Turnip', where it is the tiniest creature that makes the difference.

Choice and decision-making

Opportunities for choice-making are a familiar feature of our practice, as too is our expertise in finding a means by which students can be enabled to take an active part in this process. It is down to us to create these opportunities and, wherever possible, to extend these beyond food examples!

Equally, as students get older, we need to widen choices. Some of their peers have more choice at this age. We also need to be more creative in thinking of meaningful opportunities, particularly for students at the earliest levels, in areas such as curriculum choices, which adults or peers they work with or career choices, for example.

Specific approaches

So far, discussion has centred around general approaches to teaching and learning. This next section examines some quite specific approaches and contexts for addressing citizenship. It is hoped that practitioners can add to the creativity and flexibility of their teaching styles from these suggestions.

Circle time

Circle time is often suggested as a useful approach to citizenship. Clough and Holden (2002) agree it can be a forum for some areas, but it does not, on its own, equal citizenship education.

Curry and Bromfield (1994) maintain that circle time enables pupils to develop their unique potential; enhances self-esteem; affirms positive attributes; builds trust and confidence; demonstrates friendship skills; can be used to teach social skills; fosters a caring group feeling; and encourages cooperation. It provides a safe and supportive environment where all are valued and where personal and group issues can be examined. This is supported in the QCA schemes of work:

> Conducted in an atmosphere of trust, cooperation and mutual respect, and in conjunction with group work and role play, circle time develops communication skills and helps to develop confidence and individual and group responsibility. (QCA 2002b, Teacher's guide: 52)

A circle is used for a number of reasons: equality – all pupils can be seen and eye contact is then possible; and there are no physical barriers (tables and chairs) which helps reduce distracting behaviour. Pupils may sit anywhere in the circle, and staff, too, are included in it.

Curry and Bromfield (1994) propose these ground rules:

- only one person speaks at any time;
- we listen to the person who is speaking; and
- we have fun and make sure we don't spoil anybody else's fun.

They suggest that these can be added to with further rules as appropriate – for example the right to pass, that it is OK to make mistakes, that names are not used when a comment is negative, that confidentiality is respected, that the ideas and values of others are respected, and that pupils are responsible for their own behaviour.

Rowe (2001: 20) recommends similar rules for a *citizenship circle*:

- Only one person talks at a time
- Listen carefully and don't distract each other
- Respect what others have to say
- It's OK to disagree
- Always be prepared to give a reason for your opinion
- Try to 'follow on'; from what has just been said.

Curry and Bromfield (1994) further advise that circle time needs a consistent structure:

- a warm up game, as an energy raiser;
- a round (teaching pupils to be active listeners, ensuring that all can contribute, turn taking);
- a core activity;
- a conference, providing an opportunity to reflect and extract learning; and
- a concluding game, to reunite the group.

School Councils UK (www.schoolcouncils.org) advocate circle time as a 'developmental foundation' on which to build structures for school councils.

Use of stories and storying

The idea and value of stories or 'storying' are explored elsewhere by Lawson and Fergusson (2001). This value is based on this process being such a familiar, everyday part of sharing experiences in so many cultures. Whether it is used formally or more informally in social situations, storytelling provides a flexible tool to explore a myriad of situations, either within or beyond our personal experiences. The flexibility comes from the storyteller being in a position to emphasise or omit aspects that are significant or important to themselves or the story sequence or even to encourage response from their audience. They also have the power to alter the sequence of events completely – to fabricate the story or stray from the truth!

Rowe (2001) explains that stories provide an effective way to stimulate 'enquiry-based learning' and encourage 'joint reflection'. In engaging pupils' emotions as well as their intellect, he suggests that genuine reflection can take place. 'Stories can provide the kind of rich stimulus that a child is able to approach from a personal viewpoint. Stories are capable of taking us beneath the surface events of life to reveal motives and feelings' (*ibid.*, p. 32). Klein (2001: 19) suggests that stories can be 'a vehicle for exploring sensitive issues, thus putting a safe distance between the children and the characters so they could explore their own emotions at one remove, and not feel exposed.'

The use of stories can encourage discussion and debate, they can also prepare children for coping in other situations. In particular, the use of 'social stories' can be especially useful to help pupils prepare for and manage challenging situations – a forthcoming hospital visit, or the necessity to remain quiet during a trip to the library, for example.

There are some published schemes for PSHE and citizenship based on children's storybooks (for example, the Hopscotch series [www.hopscotch.com] and the set of *Thinkers* stories, available with Rowe 2001). Many of these are aimed at younger children. Rowe and Newton's (1994) *You, Me, Us!* resource also contains a number of useful stories. However, the notion of using a story as a tool for learning can be developed across all ages with the use of appropriate stories, whether fictional or based in real life.

For example, *The Little Red Hen*, questioning:

- Why didn't the animals want to help?
- How do you think this made the hen feel?
- When the hen said the other animals couldn't have any bread, how do you think they felt?
- Why is it important to share?
- How could we change the story so that the hen would share the bread?

(from Klein 2001: 23)

QCA support material includes a similar questioning format to support discussion of fiction. For example:

- Imagine that you are X. What do you think she/he is thinking? What reason would you give for her/his actions?
- Can you think of a similar situation in real life?
- Was X right to do that?
- Why do you think that was right/wrong?

(Drawn from QCA 2002b, Teacher's guide: 53)

There are a number of published personal life stories/narratives about the lives of people with learning difficulties. The *Living Our Lives* series (DfES 2001b) especially focuses on the person's 'experience of being accepted as a person in their own right and making choice and decisions for themselves'. St George's Hospital Medical School and the Royal College of Psychiatrists produce a series of simple stories that look at life events such as bereavement, leaving home, being arrested and speaking up for yourself. The 'Books Beyond Words' series are books with pictures which tell a story but do not have text, and are used to talk through issues in the lives of people (with learning disabilities) (www.rcpsych.ac.uk/publications/bbw).

Students can make their own stories. Low-tech ideas may, for one individual, be a series of two or three significant photographs that depict meaningful objects, people or places. More sophisticated use of ICT (e.g. PowerPoint) might create a more detailed story, where possibilities to personalise them are endless (digital images, sound clips, different symbol systems).

Story dice offer a different means of generating spontaneous story scenarios – one die for characters, one for settings and so on. The story develops through pupil contribution and random events of the dice. Dice can be developed for particular conflicts – for example bullying, not sharing, or name calling.

It can be useful to explore alternative views of stories by 'turning stories around'. For example, *Three Little Pigs*:

- Create alternative endings – death of the wolf, the wolf saying sorry to the pigs.
- Questioning – How did the wolf feel about being excluded by the pigs? Could the wolf have been misunderstood?

(from Klein 2001: 20)

Using or making interactive stories where decision-making is required can offer further opportunities. *Citizenship Issues: Assemblies About Life* (Womack 2000) is a collection of stories around social and moral themes with a choice of endings.

Use of photos, pictures and maps

Photographs and pictures have long held a valuable place in providing pupils with learning difficulties with a stimulus for learning. Visual images offer a concrete and constant reference to which pupils can attend – it does not disappear as the spoken word does. Many pupils prefer to use their visual channel to other styles of learning. Photographs and pictures may be from newspapers and magazines in addition to published teacher resources. Pupils may take their own photographs, video footage and draw their own pictures too.

One resource pack from Save the Children (2002) proffers valuable aspects afforded by using photos as:

- a focus for discussion;
- an introduction to ideas outside of personal experiences;
- a tool for developing enquiry, visual literacy and communication skills; and
- a resource or prop for an activity.

The resource continues with guidelines on using photos to encourage students to 'read' or make sense of the photos, by finding the 'symbols' or visual clues within the images, to think about the messages (hidden or otherwise). We are told to 'let the children question what they see', to focus on similarities rather than on differences. This will help students to 'make connections' with those who live in different parts of the world who may have different customs and lifestyles; in turn this will help to develop respect for diversity. The guidelines also prepare us to see that the immediacy of photos can evoke powerful emotions and to be ready to value the experiences and opinions we are offered; to see that in these types of activities there are no 'right' or 'wrong' answers.

Rowe (2001) similarly promotes the use of pictures for use with children, particularly where there may be language or communication difficulties. One advantage of their use is that 'children draw directly on their own experience or world view in interpreting them' (p. 26).

Grimwade *et al.* (2000) provide a range of ideas for using photographs, presented here with our examples for use with pupils with learning difficulties:

- questioning photographs – asking questions about a photograph;
- similarities and differences – comparing photographs, especially where they show people's contrasting lives;
- issues – What issue is depicted in the photograph? (e.g. water, child labour, education);
- sorting into sets (e.g. by issue [traffic, water] or by gender, work role differences or consequence [war-injury, homelessness, poverty]);
- speech bubbles – What might the people be saying?;
- captions – devise captions to go with photographs; they could offer different perspectives (e.g. a photo of a group of climbers on Everest could have a caption for a holiday company, a message about tourists boosting a local economy, a list of ways in which they are damaging this environment or, a good example of cross-cultural collaboration); and
- look at me – place a photograph or drawing of the pupil on a photograph of another place; ask the pupil to think about what it might feel like to be there.

Role play and puppets

> Role play is not about performance or performing – it is a method by which children are able to explore personal and social experience. Role play is used to explore: how different people behave, in ways that are perceived to be good or bad; different ways of life; having different beliefs; being of different social standing in society; expressing contrasting opinions; and revealing a range of feelings and emotions. (QCA 2002b, Teacher's guide: 51)

This approach, as opposed to storytelling, can be a very difficult concept for pupils with learning difficulties especially. From one perspective, they may not have had experience of the type of scenario they are involved in role-playing and may therefore find it very difficult to predict how to portray a character or their behaviour. A different perspective raises the difficulty of being able to 'imagine' themselves 'in role'; to distinguish between real and fictional life. Is this an activity or an 'event' in its own right?

Puppets can provide anonymity. Some individuals prefer to interact with a less 'human' or more detached 'other' – for example some students on the autistic spectrum. Puppets provide something to focus on – some with provision to use signing or mouth movements (puppets which utilise the puppeteer's hands as 'their own'). Puppets are of interest to all ages and can be age-appropriate across the phases.

Board games and scenario boards

Either commercially produced or adapted versions can provide a focus to explore issues. Games can introduce both random and selected outcomes, again allowing opportunities to gain a wider understanding. Scenario boards or symbol boards with potential key symbols or pictures can enable students to think about or select sequences of events and their possible consequences. Games can help to reinforce messages of active citizenship. For example, a board game with a focus on waste was developed by the Institute for Citizenship (2002) project, with gains around the board being given for thoughtful disposal or recycling of waste.

Discussion

Discussion skills need specific teaching and opportunities for regular practice. Ground rules, for example, like those for circle time, may need to be established and should come from the pupils themselves. Questioning skills also need teaching and practice. Rowe (2001) suggests that pupils are encouraged to ask questions after a story is read, these are listed and pupils vote on which questions to examine and in which order. The *Who, What, When, How* and *Why?* questions provide a firm basis. He also provides a number of teacher questions to improve children's understanding and enrich discussion (for example, What do you think about...? What would you do if...?) and to promote moral awareness (for example, Do you think that is fair? Why? Why not? How do you think s/he was feeling?). He states that

> better quality discussion is likely to develop when teachers:
> - Talk less
> - Ask fewer but more open questions
> - Share in the enquiry with the children, modelling reflective thinking
> - Avoid commenting on what a child says; but, instead, offer it to the group to respond

- Give the children more time to think, pausing longer between questions.

(Rowe 2001: 22)

Newspaper articles, especially those with a strong pictorial or photographic element, can provide topical themes for discussion and debate. Pupils may bring articles into school and pupils may vote on which issue to examine. Perspectives from different newspapers can provide an additional focus for discussion.

Making decisions, dilemmas and debate

Dilemma game

Klein (2001: 35) describes a dilemma game to stimulate discussion. This starts from statements, for example, 'you should always do what an adult tells you' or 'children of your age should go to bed at nine', and pupils have to say whether they agree, strongly agree, disagree or strongly disagree. This also helps demonstrate to pupils that situations are rarely black and white.

Yes/no interlude

Klein also describes a 'Yes/no interlude' (p. 37) where two opposite corners of the room are designated YES and NO and pupils position themselves on a line between the two corners according to how strongly they agree or disagree with a statement. This could be following a story. Klein suggests some questions for *Cinderella*, e.g. Was it fair that Cinderella did all the work? Should she have gone to the ball?

'Yes/no' could be simplified by just having a choice of yes or no rather than a continuum, enabling questions to be more straightforward; for example, Do you like ice-cream?

The great divide... you just decide (from Clough and Holden 2002: 66–7)

This is a means of helping decision-making, encouraging pupils to express their views in a structured way without the need for speech. A rope is placed in a straight line down the middle of the classroom as 'the great divide'. One side of the line represents 'I agree', the other side 'I disagree', or 'Yes' and 'No'. Pupils move to either side of the line according to their view about a statement. Choices need not necessarily be explained. However, Clough and Holden suggest using a 'power ball' (perhaps an inflatable globe) to throw to pupils who do wish to comment on their choice.

Statements can be simple. Clough and Holden suggest: 'Red is a nicer colour than blue'; 'Dogs are better than cats'. Symbols and photographs can be used to facilitate understanding. The statements can be simplified or made more complex, as appropriate to the needs of the pupils. For example: 'Swimming is nice' or 'I feel happy today', as opposed to 'Science is the best subject at school' or '*Eastenders* is more true to life than *Neighbours*'.

Debate

Debates are more formalised forms of discussion and have their own rules and running order. Gregory (2002) lists the rules of a debate for children:

- All children must sit quietly and listen to the speaker;

- There are two sides – Side A and Side B – and they take it in turns to speak;
- Children in the audience are not allowed to discuss their opinions about what the speakers have said;
- All children in the audience have one vote. They will be asked to vote at the end of the debate by the chairperson. The children speaking in the debate are not allowed to vote;
- Children do not have to vote. If they choose not to, they are called 'abstainers'. The number of votes for each side and the number of abstainers will be announced by the chairperson at the end of the debate;
- It is polite to clap at the end of each speech, even if you do not agree with what the speaker has said.

A suggested 'running order' of debates is presented in Chapter 5.

Gregory suggests debates on well-known stories and tales; for example, which of the ugly sisters should be made to do the housework when Cinderella has left to marry Prince Charming!

Pros and cons (from Miller 1997: 60)

Miller describes this as 'a way of exploring several different options and considering the possible benefits and problems of each one'. For example, choosing between two activities – one which involves everybody or one which can be played only by two people at a time. Initially pupils can be asked which they would prefer. Then, using a large sheet of paper divided into four equal parts, encourage the pupils to consider good and bad/positive and negative things about each choice (see Figure 4.1). Ask them to make their choice again. Have any pupils changed their mind? Why?

Choice A Good things	Choice B Good things
Choice A Bad things	Choice B Bad things

Figure 4.1 Pros and cons (from Miller 1997: 60)

Visitors and visits

Earlier in this chapter, we highlighted the need, wherever possible, to strive for meaningful contexts. The value of visiting places as the centre of learning needs no reinforcement, but it may be worth exploring the assumptions of student experience we unwittingly make. Visiting the homes of classmates or staff to experience similarities and differences is likely to have more impact than solely handling artefacts. Visits, for example, to the local council chamber, religious buildings or leisure facilities can put what they have learnt into context. Sequenced visits can offer progression and are also useful to add to the greater scheme of things. For example, to follow a (food) chain:

> farm – collection – packing – delivery – shop – restaurant.

To focus further, visits from people who are actively part of these places or communities also help add to the bigger picture. For example visits from a local Iman, someone from the Salvation Army, a magistrate, a police officer, a fire service official, a member of a local charity, an MP, a school crossing person, a town crier or a mayoress. Pupils may prepare questions in advance and may video or photograph the interview/presentation. They may also need an opportunity to examine artefacts connected with the roles of visitors.

Information technology

Almost every aspect of access to citizenship can be supported or enhanced by ICT in some way, but can in no way replace the role of people. Technology offers a means to create personalised routes to learning – stories about individuals, school newspapers, 'messages' for assemblies and a means to share and celebrate achievements. These are all improved by the ability to import familiar images or other preferred and accessible formats (photos, symbols, video clips, text, sound clips). This strategy offers access to choice and decision-making, giving students a voice – literally via speech output devices. The interactive options can be easily created by ICT – opportunities to be flexible in creating or sequencing events or stories, for example, by having random or optional endings or choices. In addition, use of the internet and email can add a further dimension (see Useful websites). They can enable meaningful interactivity, communication and exchange within and between classrooms, or with much more distant places!

CHAPTER FIVE

Citizenship activities

Introduction

In this chapter a wide range of ideas, activities and resources is presented to begin to address the many aspects of citizenship and PSHE identified within this book.

Staff working within the area of learning difficulties are, by demand, extraordinarily creative in responding to the diverse needs of their pupils. It is hoped that the many ideas contained here are presented in an accessible form, but also that they will persist in inspiring that creativity.

The greater part of these ideas originate from current practice in schools, or work generated from practitioners involved in the development of materials for schools through sponsored projects (such as the Institute for Citizenship (IfC) 2002 or QCA 2001a, 2001b, 2001c). We are extremely grateful to these individuals, schools and projects for their willingness to share and develop good practice in meeting the needs of pupils with learning difficulties and the challenges of citizenship.

As previously stated, there are strong overlaps between Chapters 4, 5 and 6. It is therefore advisable to gain an overview of these three. Similarly, some of the practical teaching and learning approaches presented here may have been placed under one heading, but will also provide excellent and flexible tools for use in other areas.

For ease of access, we have divided the activities and ideas under four main headings:

- Social and moral responsibility/rights and responsibilities
  - self and others
  - rules
  - responsibilities
  - collaborative work
  - choices
  - conflict and conflict resolution
  - social and moral dilemmas
  - rights
- Community involvement/communities and identity
  - identity
  - different identities and diversity
  - school community
  - local community
  - wider community and global community
  - environmental issues
- Political literacy
  - decision-making
  - laws
  - government
  - voting and elections

- – economy
- – media
- – public services
- School councils – this area is fully explored in Chapter 6.

There will be overlaps with the many areas and ideas presented here, although these are not always acknowledged explicitly.

Social and moral responsibility/rights and responsibilities

Self and others

Expressing self

Emotion photos and symbols can be used to help pupils identify feelings. Some emotion symbols are reproduced in the IfC (2002) resource. Puppets can be another way of facilitating this.

Mirror, mirror (Hill 2001)

Try to mirror exactly the facial expressions, movements or posture of someone else, either by facing each other or, where possible, by both facing a mirror. Move on to 'passing round' an expression or action, e.g. smile, patting arm or nodding head.

Giving permission

The Image in Action publications (Scott 1994; Johns *et al.* 2001) include a number of drama activities for students with severe and profound and multiple learning difficulties as part of sex and relationships education. These activities include those about giving permission – 'Would you like to wear my hat?' 'Can I touch your arm?'

Can we come closer?

A variation on a traditional game, *May I?*, to give practice in establishing and maintaining boundaries. One person is in the middle of an open space; the others scatter. They ask 'Can we come closer?' The person in the middle says 'Yes, __ steps' (number of steps closer) or 'No, __ steps back' (number of steps away from the person in the middle). This back-and-forth process continues until the person in the middle answers 'You are all just right'. The circle scatters and the next person takes a turn.

Ourselves topic

This is an example from *Planning, Teaching and Assessing the Curriculum for Pupils with Learning Difficulties: PSHE and Citizenship for Key Stage 1:*

Pupils develop awareness of themselves and their bodies. They may:

- take photographs of staff and pupils and use name cards and photographs to consider who is in their class. They match these to people, sort them into boys and girls, play 'Guess who?' games with them;
- make 'Who am I?' posters – for example, choosing their favourite photographs and colours; describing their preferred method of communication;
- observe and examine faces by looking in mirrors, by looking at pictures and

making happy, sad and angry faces. They have their faces painted. They position the features of a face using a touch screen with a computer program, a velcro face and a paper plate face;

• take part in body awareness activities – for example, by experiencing a range of different positions, supported by equipment or a person if necessary; performing action songs that highlight main body parts; by taking part in movement, dance or swimming activities.

(QCA 2001c: 12)

Council of All Beings (developed from Hicks 2001: 49–53)

This activity aims to develop awareness and compassion for all living things:

1. It is carried out in a large space, for example, the school hall. Pupils find a space to sit or lie. A tape/CD of 'natural' sounds provides background sounds, e.g. wind, sea, animal sounds. Pupils think about and choose a creature they would like to represent.

2. In the classroom, pupils research their creature – habits, size, shape, colours, dangers, special qualities. Pupils practise moving like their creature. They make a plan of the face for face painting or make masks.

   They consider how they, as their creature, would like to appear at the Council. Practise what they might communicate to humans about themselves – how does it feel to be this creature? What are their specific strengths and qualities?

3. Council of All Beings

   The Council is held in a large circle. A member of staff could be the representative for human beings. It could take a number of formats, for example:

   • each creature takes it in turns to present themselves;
   • each creature may communicate what is happening to them as a result of human actions;
   • each creature names a particular gift they would like to give to humans, e.g. butterfly might offer lightness of touch.

   Council could end with music, laughter, animal calls or silence.

Rules

Sabotage of traditional games with rules – for example board games and football – can help to demonstrate the need for rules such as turn-taking.

Class rules

Figure 5.1 shows the Year 11 class rules at Montacute School which the students developed with some support.

Fishing game (from Miller 1997)

The rules for a given situation (e.g. class or school rules) are each written or depicted on card fish shapes. Some rules not appropriate to this situation are also included. Each fish needs a paper clip attached to it and they are put into a box (or net). Fishing rods

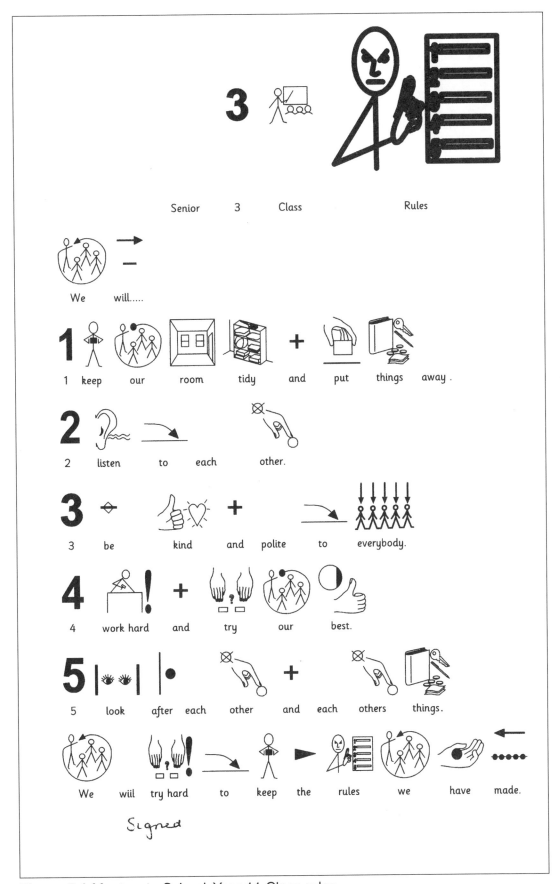

Figure 5.1 Montacute School: Year 11 Class rules

(dowels, string and magnets) are also needed. Pupils take it in turns to 'fish a rule'. The rule can be discussed – is it a rule for the given situation? Why do we have that rule? What does it mean? If it is not a rule that belongs to the situation, it is returned to the box/net.

Rules in different situations (from IfC 2002, Government)

Consider rules that apply to different in-school and out-of-school places – for example, rules for the dining-room, rules for the food technology room, rules for crossing the road, rules at home. Some rules are more explicit than others.

Pupils could match rules for different situations with a photograph/picture/symbol of that place or situation, e.g. make your bed – home; wear uniform – school. They could also consider who makes those rules: parents/family; school (who in school – headteacher, governors, school council?); the government.

They could also look at the consequences of rule-breaking.

Responsibilities

Taking and sharing responsibility

This example is from *Planning, Teaching and Assessing the Curriculum for Pupils with Learning Difficulties: PSHE and Citizenship.* Pupils may

- take part in class rotas, by sharing jobs or carrying them out independently, for example, carrying the register to the office, tidying the book corner;
- recognise and carry their own coat and bag and other personal belongings;
- borrow, take home, then return, the class photograph album;
- lead the way to different areas in the school and show visitors around the school;
- take messages to different parts of the school.

(QCA 2001c: 8)

Story: William and the Guinea-Pig, *by Gill Rose (Citizenship Foundation Thinkers series)*

This is a story about the responsibility of caring for an animal.

Jobs rota

Jobs can be assigned to pairs or groups of children so that all children have jobs (and support as appropriate). Rotas can use a variety of sensory channels – for example making use of photos, symbols, objects or audiotapes.

Roles within the class/school

- class 'monitor' (assigned specific tasks, e.g. register pupils, take dinner numbers, water plants, tidy away, choose music for end of day)
- lunchtime helpers
- playground buddies
- playground monitors
- story reader to younger children

- ICT technicians
- assistant caretakers
- class/school photographer
- peer supporter
- peer mediator
- group responsibility for display

Class monitors and prefects

At Montacute School some older pupils are class monitors and help classes of younger pupils. They meet the class staff to find out how they can help and get to know the pupils in the class. At assembly time they escort the children, sit with them and accompany them to the front of assembly if support is required. Some class monitors attend their class's circle time sessions. They may also represent their class on the School Council.

Montacute School also has prefects. Their list of roles and responsibilities was drawn up and decided by pupils and staff:

- to be a helpful and caring member of our school – helping younger children and the more vulnerable children at lunchtimes, playtimes, assembly times, in the corridor coming into and going from school; help any member of staff when needed;
- to be aware of the school environment, making sure it is tidy and safe;
- to assist when visitors come into school, welcoming, serving teas, etc.;
- to try to be polite at all times;
- to alert staff if there are problems;
- to be a responsible member of our school and be a good role model for younger members of our school.

Collaborative work

This might include, for example, paired work (various combinations of age, ability, level of participation and responsibility), paired reading, group work, buddying and peer support.

Mencap Transactive project (www.trans-active.org.uk)

The *Transactive* project is an example of collaborative work between pupils with learning difficulties and peer supporters from a mainstream setting. Each pupil has made a 'personal passport' as a multimedia project using PowerPoint. This is comprised of their favourite object, favourite clothing, favourite place, special ability and special friend. It has involved pupils making choices and decisions and 'having a say' about their life and future wishes. The passports can be used as part of the transition planning process. The project has been piloted in the Birmingham and Lichfield areas with a national launch in spring 2003.

Choices

Pupils/students may consider the choices available to them in their life. Can they choose, for example:

- the time they get up;

- what they eat for breakfast;
- what they wear;
- who their friends are;
- how much pocket money they receive and how they can spend it?

The *Self-Advocacy Action Pack* (DfES 2001c: 129–31) examines the importance of making choices and decisions for students with learning difficulties as adults:

> Making your own choices and decisions is an important part of having control over what happens in your life. There are many different choices and decisions to make:
>
> - choosing which friends you have
> - choosing which college or centre you go to
> - deciding what jobs you want
> - choices of what you can do, not being told
> - making choices about where to go on holiday
> - deciding what to wear each day
> - making choices about where to live.

Conflict and conflict resolution

This involves raising awareness to feelings and acknowledging a range of different feelings and emotions attached to them, both in one's self and in others.

Social stories

These are individualised stories that address aspects of behaviour and the consequences and feelings they may produce, followed by some suggestions of more appropriate or alternative ways of behaving. These stories are written with, and for, one individual and are set within a context that the individual can relate to. This idea of personalising scenarios can be further developed for more general issues or for a wider group.

Scenarios

Some examples are included in *Citizenship Education for Young People with Special Educational Needs* (IfC 2002, 'Conflict Resolution' section). They include photographs of situations where conflict may arise – for example sharing crisps – and the possible consequences. Additionally there are 'win–win' scenarios with choices of words for speech bubbles – for example two young people, one wishing to watch a film on television and the other a cartoon.

Story: Tusk Tusk, *by David McKee*

This is a picture-book story of a group of elephants which were black or white in colour. They did not trust each other and argued, fought and killed each other, but both the black and the white peace-loving elephants escaped into the jungle. Eventually, years later, their descendants, which were grey in colour, came out of the jungle and lived in peace, until they began to notice other differences between themselves.

The story could be used to explore issues of intolerance, diversity, racism, war and peace.

Conflict around the school

How and why conflicts happen – pupils take photographs of places around school and artificially set up incidents.

Social and moral dilemmas

This is an example from *Planning, Teaching and Assessing the Curriculum for Pupils with Learning Difficulties: PSHE and Citizenship* for Key Stage 2:

> As part of their regular classroom routines at Key Stage 2, pupils have opportunities to take part in discussions where any contribution or expression of preference is valid. They may consider social and moral dilemmas that they come across in everyday life – for example, the need to tidy up the classroom so people can move around safely, and issues of right and wrong, and fairness, such as how to share out the last piece of cake. (QCA 2001c: 16)

Stories

As examined in Chapter 4, stories provide a particular 'way in' to more abstract or inaccessible experiences or situations, especially social and moral issues.

Fictional published stories for younger pupils, for example:

- listening to each other – *Not Now, Bernard*, by David McKee
- making difficult choices – *The Rainbow Fish*, by Marcus Pfister
- coping with prejudice – *Amazing Grace*, by Mary Hoffman
- empathising – *Big Brother, Little Brother*, by Penny Dale
- making new friends – *The Gotcha Smile*, by Rita Mitchell and Alex Ayliffe.

Other 'stories' may include:

- TV soaps, *Big Brother/Pop Idol*-style shows;
- everyday life stories – personal, local or topical;
- social stories – scripts that can help prepare for and manage challenging situations;
- drama – 'what if…?' scenarios;
- puppet shows;
- before and after photos, adding speech bubbles on photos;
- artefacts or props – detective work/problem-solving – who does this handbag belong to?, using clues from the contents of the bag;
- ICT decision-making scenarios.

Role play

It is important to be cautious in the use of role play with pupils with learning difficulties (see concerns expressed in Chapter 4).

Grimwade *et al.* (2000: 25) suggest a role play activity concerning the building of a hotel complex on an unspoilt, tropical beach. The pupils role play the different groups of people who might use the beach, e.g. fisherfolk, children, local resident, travel company rep, holidaymaker. They may wear appropriate clothes or carry an appropriate object to represent their role. What do they do on the beach? Are they rich or poor? Do they live there? Do they work there? Do they play there or use the beach for leisure? What effect might a hotel complex have on their lives? They could vote for the development to go ahead or stop it.

Fairness

A number of activities, when used with caution and careful thought, can provoke discussion about fairness. For example:

- how to share out the last piece of cake;

- only giving snacks to pupils with blue eyes;

- using different colour T-shirts in drama and treating each group differently;

- deliberate provocation from head teacher – e.g. 'no more swimming'; 'no more parties on birthdays'; 'only brown-eyed children allowed in the playground'.

Values

Focus on one identified value per week/month (e.g. honesty, kindness, courage), so everyone becomes aware of this, recognises what it looks like in practice and actively shares in the experience.

Rights

Self-advocacy groups for people with learning difficulties have described rights: 'Rights are about things you want to do in your life and the way you want to be treated. The right to speak up. The right not to be bullied. The right to vote' (DfES 2001c: 46).

They continue: 'Having rights does not just mean getting what you want. Other people have rights and it is important to take notice of them. For example, if you expect people to treat you with respect, they will expect you to treat them with respect too' (*ibid.*, p. 49).

Pupil/student charter

NIACE (The National Organisation for Adult Learning), working with adult students with learning difficulties, has produced the following Charter for Learning, reproduced with pictorial support in the *Self-Advocacy Action Pack* (DfES 2001c: 58–9):

Students with learning difficulties want:

- the right to speak up
- the right to choose to go to classes
- the right to have support
- the right to have the chance to make friends
- the right to have fun learning
- the right to good access
- the right not to be bullied
- the right to be treated as adults with respect
- the right to have clear information that we can understand
- the right to have good teaching
- the right to be able to do a course to get a job
- the right to learn in a nice place

Students may consider their rights and entitlements. For example, St George's School display, in the entrance, their School Charter, which is for students and staff:

- Everyone has the right to take part in school activities irrespective of their special needs or their gender.
- Religious beliefs and cultural backgrounds are to be valued.
- We must be sensitive to each other's needs and feelings so that we endeavour to respond appropriately.
- We want to encourage people to try new experiences and allow them to make mistakes in a supportive environment.
- We should be familiar with and accept the ways in which we communicate and be ready to communicate more effectively.

Staff charters were considered in Chapter 3.

Needs and wants (adapted from Klein 2001: 17)

Collect a range of photographs depicting basic human needs (e.g. food, water, shelter, school) among a range of other photographs (e.g. CDs, designer clothes). Sort photographs into 'needs' and 'wants'. The UNICEF UK's youth rights website (see Useful websites) has a pictorial card game to distinguish wants from needs.

UN Convention on the Rights of the Child (United Nations 1989)

Below is a simplified version for children (adapted by Lina Fajerman of Save the Children, in Klein 2001: 14). *A life like mine* (UNICEF 2002) is a colour photo book version illustrating these rights:

Article 3:	Grown ups should do their best for you
Article 6:	You have the right to life
Article 12:	Grown ups must listen to what children say
Article 13:	You can say what you think
Article 14:	You have a right to your religion
Article 15:	You can make friends with whomever you choose
Article 16:	You can have your own private things (diary)
Article 17:	No one must tell lies about you
Article 18:	Parents must take care of their children
Article 19:	Children must not be hurt
Article 20:	Someone must look after children
Article 22:	Refugee children must be looked after
Article 23:	Disabled children need to have special care
Article 24:	Children must have medicine if they are sick
Article 25:	You should have food, clothes and a place to live
Article 28:	All children should go to school and have an education
Article 31:	Children have a right to play
Article 32:	Children shouldn't have to do work that hurts them
Article 33:	You should be safe from drugs

Human rights

A simplified version of the Universal Declaration of Human Rights is available at www.savethechildren.org.uk/partners/

Part of this Save the Children website includes a matching game http://www.savethechildren.org.uk/eyetoeye/, matching the appropriate human right to a photograph, e.g. matching the appropriate photograph to 'You have the right to play and relax by doing things like sports, music and drama'. Another section of the website involves an activity matching photos to written descriptions of the articles of the UN Convention on the Rights of the Child.

Animal rights (from IfC 2002, Rights and responsibilities)

Pupils can study animal needs and care. Pupils could care for a class pet. What do different pets need? (e.g. shelter, food, water, bed, exercise, love).

Consumer rights (from IfC 2002, Rights and responsibilities)

Suggestions here include expectations when you buy something, through role play, for example, buying broken items, burnt toast. Trading Standards staff may display confiscated goods which are counterfeit or unsafe – can pupils spot the fake items and the reasons for being unsafe?

Community involvement/communities and identity

As noted in Chapter 4, the notion of community is not straightforward for many pupils with learning difficulties. The school's local community may not be their home neighbourhood community, as many students travel a substantial distance to school. The concept of a wider community may be complex. It is essential, however, to view pupils as citizens who participate actively in a community. In addition, we need to acknowledge and respond to the fact that adults are the gatekeepers to this.

Community involvement also implies schools creating and developing links with their local communities, including building successful links with parents. It is important to ask, 'Does our community involvement benefit other people? Is it mutually beneficial?'

Identity

Self-identity

A wide range of activities could be used to develop the whole sense of self – for example:

- ourselves projects – as in rights and responsibilities above;
- likes and dislikes;
- personal flags/coat of arms or markers.

There are strong links with PSHE and the personal development strand here. The spectrum encompasses individual identity through to world identity.

Toys and treasures (Hill 2001)

Share personal or family treasures – toys, ornaments, souvenirs, music, heirlooms and special gifts. Find out why they are special to that person.

Different identities and diversity

Self-awareness – Web of Likes (from Hill 2001)

This uses pupils' knowledge of their personal preferences, likes/dislikes.

Form a circle and create a web of interconnections, using a ball of wool. To start, the first person holding the wool tells the group, 'I like …' [an activity or pop idol for example] 'Who else likes …?' That person holds on to the end of the wool and then rolls the ball to someone who also likes that activity. That person then says, 'I like …' [another activity] 'Who else likes …?' This is repeated. As the game progresses the pupils will become connected by a web of yarn. As someone tugs the yarn, pupils experience physically that other people are affected. Building the web allows us to see and learn about our connections to each other; how we are linked by our many similarities and differences.

Same and different (from IfC 2002, Groups and identity)

A number of cards illustrating different criteria are used to play a game where the pupils reassemble according to the criteria and make different groups, e.g. boys/girls; wearing trainers/not wearing trainers; blue jumpers/not blue jumpers; wearing glasses/not wearing glasses. They could position themselves within chalk circles on the floor or move to different corners of the room. Photographs could be taken of the different groups and used to demonstrate that everyone is a member of different groups with different sets of people. Some criteria may include all pupils, e.g. need to eat food, need to sleep, like having friends.

The platypus story (from IfC 2002, Groups and identity)

In the beginning of time there were three tribes – the fish, the birds and the animals – who argued constantly about which group was best. The platypus did not belong to any group at all, and the fish, the birds and the animals all wanted him to join them. They called a meeting to decide. The animals said, 'We are the strongest so we are the best, brother platypus. Join us as you have fur like an animal.'

The birds said, 'Brother, you have feet and a bill like a duck and you lay eggs. You should join us. We can fly and surely we are the best?'

The fish called out to the platypus saying, 'Brother, you must join our tribe. Not only can we swim faster than the others but we can also stay underwater. They can't do that and you swim with us every day, so you know we are the best.'

The platypus listened to each group and when they had finished he said, 'I will think about what you have said and in a short time I will tell you my answer.'

A little later, the animals, the birds and the fish gathered outside the hole by the river where the platypus lived, and out came the clever little creature and said, 'I will not join ANY of you as a separate group but I will join ALL of you, as no group is any better than another, and, like me,' said the platypus, 'you are all special in your very own way.'

Institute for Citizenship 2002, Groups and identity: 8

A multimedia version of this story is available at: www.newagemultimedia.com/firebrace/platypus.html. The story can be used in a number of ways with pupils – for example: with multisensory props and experience; as a debate; to consider, categorise and sort different sorts of animals.

Rap (from IfC 2002, Diversity and identity)

A rap to celebrate individuality and difference is suggested in these resource materials:

> I have a friend, his name is Sam,
> He likes footie and strawberry jam,
> Sam is tops, he's here today,
> Sam's in the group and he's OK.
> I have a friend, her name is Sarah . . . [etc.]

Tribes (from the Citizenship Foundation [www.citfou.org.uk])

This focuses on the concept of communities working together. Students create countries or 'tribes' over a series of weeks, developing features that are important and unique to that group of people – name, symbol, laws, etc. A natural disaster then forces them to live and work with other tribes and negotiations are necessary.

School community

Pupils can participate as members of the school community in a huge variety of ways. They can:

- run a school newspaper;
- greet people as they arrive in assembly;
- be members of sports teams and represent the school at sports meetings;
- contribute to and/or attend school council meetings and take part in decision-making about school-based activities;
- run mini-enterprise schemes – for example, investigating the market for a product and selling it in the school;
- choose the music for school concerts;
- take part in public performances – for example drama, art exhibitions and school open days.

School community groups (adapted from IfC 2002, Community and voluntary groups, section 1)

Pupils may visit and record – through photography, tape recording or video – other groups within the school community (e.g. other classes, kitchen staff, football team, administrative staff, midday supervisors, senior management team, transport drivers and escorts), then examine the constituency and the roles and responsibilities of these groups:

- Who belongs to which group?
- Can you belong to more than one group?
- Which groups do you belong to?
- Which groups do you prefer?

Pupils could match artefacts and objects with the different groups. They could examine evidence (e.g. the contents of a bag) and determine from which group(s) the person belongs.

My school, my future (based on My town, my future in Clough and Holden 2002: 52)

This activity is concerned with planning the school for the future, considering the physical and social needs of the school community. The activity commences with discussion about what makes a good school and what facilities are needed. Pupils can act as advocates/interpreters for all members of the school community where appropriate. The requirements and wishes of all – pupils, staff (teachers, assistants, administration, head teacher, caretaker, kitchen staff), parents, local community – need to be considered.

- What do we like about our school?
- What would we choose to show visitors?
- Which areas need improving?
- What is currently being planned?
- What do we need here that we don't have?

This activity is, of course, most powerful and appropriate when meaningful change can actually be facilitated.

Local community

A range of local community networks and links can be established. For example:

- mainstream school links;
- adopting a local charity, taking part in fundraising activities and finding out what the money is being used for;
- investigating local voluntary groups – what is there/what do they do; what is a volunteer; can I be one; in school?
- work experience or work shadowing;
- intergenerational activities;
- business links;
- community arts events or links with a local theatre.

A living map (from Clough and Holden 2002: 51)

This activity involves drawing or building a map of the local community area with all the pupils' homes identified on it. This could be two- or three-dimensional. The homes could be identified using the pupils' photographs. Other natural and built elements need to be included too – for example, rivers, fields, hills, churches, shops. The community could be the school and its local surroundings, if more appropriate. Distinguish between the different classrooms, hall, offices and play areas.

The map can be used in a number of different ways:

- It may assist pupils in learning about the physical community – what different parts there are; what areas we use, and for what?
- it may be used, as Clough and Holden (2002) suggest, to consider things which change regularly during the year, marking these in some way and following them over a period of time – the *living* map. They include the following example: 'Julie's mother is pregnant so next to her house we place a symbol of a big belly and when her mother gives birth, we change the symbol for a new baby symbol' (p. 51);
- there are opportunities for geographical and historical investigations through such a map.

The world of work in the community (from Clough and Holden 2002: 55 and QCA 2000c)

This activity is to help pupils understand that many types of work are undertaken in the community and the various contributions made by different people through their work. This can be, again, the school community or the local community around the school.

Clough and Holden (2002: 57) provide line-drawn, photocopiable pictures of different jobs within the community (e.g. doctor, teacher, bus driver, refuse collector, shop assistant, childminder). These are also available as photographs through many careers resources for pupils with special educational needs. The photographs and drawings can be used to enable discussion about the different roles within the community and to consider issues of importance. Which job is most important, and why? The different jobs can be placed on the community map (see above) to indicate where the jobs are in the local community.

Pupils could use sensory 'job boxes' to explore artefacts associated with different jobs and use them as evidence to work out who the box belongs to.

They could meet people who work in the school and local community and investigate their jobs (e.g. the school secretary, the caretaker, a nurse, a police officer, a local religious leader, a shop assistant, a fire-fighter). This could involve visits outside school or visitors coming to the school. Pupils could prepare questions and, during an interview and visit, record with sound and digital camera images and make a book, website or PowerPoint presentation about the job.

A school in Ireland has compiled a website about jobs in their community using video clips, photographs and sound (http://www.knockevin.com/people_who_help_us.htm).

At the heart of the community

Potter (2002) provides the example of Marshfields School, a school for children with moderate learning difficulties, aged 5–18 years. The school worked with Community Service Volunteer staff to move 'from fortress to open house' and 'from suspicion to trust' in striving to be 'at the heart of the community'. Figures 5.2 and 5.3 demonstrate the involvement of the community in Marshfields and, vice versa, the involvement of Marshfield in the community.

Wider community and global community

Where in the World is Barnaby Bear?, or equivalent

This is a primary school geography activity which has many accompanying resources, including big books. A soft toy bear is followed on its journeys to different localities. Staff and pupils may take it on their holidays and send postcards and photographs from different places. Pupils learn about those places through Barnaby's travels and experiences.

Flat Stanley Project

This activity is linked through the 'Montage Plus' section of the British Council website (www.britishcouncil.org/education/schools/index.htm)

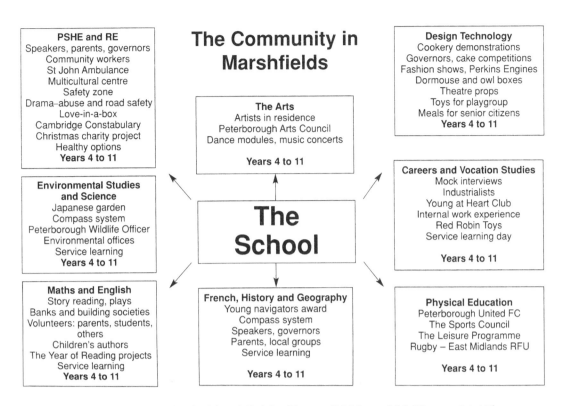

The Community in Marshfields

PSHE and RE
Speakers, parents, governors
Community workers
St John Ambulance
Multicultural centre
Safety zone
Drama–abuse and road safety
Love-in-a-box
Cambridge Constabulary
Christmas charity project
Healthy options
Years 4 to 11

Environmental Studies and Science
Japanese garden
Compass system
Peterborough Wildlife Officer
Environmental offices
Service learning
Years 4 to 11

Maths and English
Story reading, plays
Banks and building societies
Volunteers: parents, students, others
Children's authors
The Year of Reading projects
Service learning
Years 4 to 11

The Arts
Artists in residence
Peterborough Arts Council
Dance modules, music concerts
Years 4 to 11

The School

French, History and Geography
Young navigators award
Compass system
Speakers, governors
Parents, local groups
Service learning
Years 4 to 11

Design Technology
Cookery demonstrations
Governors, cake competitions
Fashion shows, Perkins Engines
Dormouse and owl boxes
Theatre props
Toys for playgroup
Meals for senior citizens
Years 4 to 11

Careers and Vocation Studies
Mock interviews
Industrialists
Young at Heart Club
Internal work experience
Red Robin Toys
Service learning day
Years 4 to 11

Physical Education
Peterborough United FC
The Sports Council
The Leisure Programme
Rugby – East Midlands RFU
Years 4 to 11

Figure 5.2 The community in Marshfields (Potter 2002, p. 262 Figure 14.13)

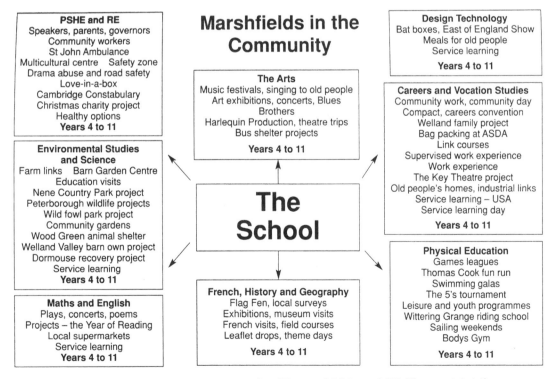

Marshfields in the Community

PSHE and RE
Speakers, parents, governors
Community workers
St John Ambulance
Multicultural centre   Safety zone
Drama abuse and road safety
Love-in-a-box
Cambridge Constabulary
Christmas charity project
Healthy options
Years 4 to 11

Environmental Studies and Science
Farm links   Barn Garden Centre
Education visits
Nene Country Park project
Peterborough wildlife projects
Wild fowl park project
Community gardens
Wood Green animal shelter
Welland Valley barn own project
Dormouse recovery project
Service learning
Years 4 to 11

Maths and English
Plays, concerts, poems
Projects – the Year of Reading
Local supermarkets
Service learning
Years 4 to 11

The Arts
Music festivals, singing to old people
Art exhibitions, concerts, Blues Brothers
Harlequin Production, theatre trips
Bus shelter projects
Years 4 to 11

The School

French, History and Geography
Flag Fen, local surveys
Exhibitions, museum visits
French visits, field courses
Leaflet drops, theme days
Years 4 to 11

Design Technology
Bat boxes, East of England Show
Meals for old people
Service learning
Years 4 to 11

Careers and Vocation Studies
Community work, community day
Compact, careers convention
Welland family project
Bag packing at ASDA
Link courses
Supervised work experience
Work experience
The Key Theatre project
Old people's homes, industrial links
Service learning – USA
Service learning day
Years 4 to 11

Physical Education
Games leagues
Thomas Cook fun run
Swimming galas
The 5's tournament
Leisure and youth programmes
Wittering Grange riding school
Sailing weekends
Bodys Gym
Years 4 to 11

Figure 5.3 Marshfields in the community (Potter 2002, p. 263 Figure 14.14)

Figure 5.4 Flat Stanley (from http://flatstanley.enoreo.on.ca/index.htm)

This is an uncomplicated activity, similar to *Barnaby Bear*. Students make a paper 'Flat Stanley' and mail it, along with a blank journal, to someone on the list of participants, or to a celebrity or politician. The recipient treats the visiting Stanley as a guest and takes it to various places. After a few weeks, Stanley is mailed back with a completed journal and perhaps some photographs, postcards and souvenirs. You share with your class what Stanley has done and where he has been, and plot his travels on a map. Some classes send out hundreds of Stanleys. Having your class on the list means being prepared to have others send Stanleys to you too. The *Flat Stanley* site includes curriculum connections and details on how to make the most of this activity.

Twin towns and exchanges

Links may be made between schools and places in the same country but in a contrasting locality or with schools and places in other countries. As Davies points out, 'Classes who carry out exchanges with schools in contrasting localities in Britain or in other European countries have the opportunity to compare the nature and advantages and disadvantages of living in alternative communities' (Davies 1996: 123).

The British Council supports many projects for pupils with special educational needs in international activity, particularly aiming to develop cultural awareness and understanding. This includes, for example, exchange visits, partner schools, joint curriculum initiatives (http://www.britishcouncil.org/education/schools/index.htm).

> Critchill School in Frome, Somerset, is a small school for 4–16-year-olds with moderate, severe and profound and multiple learning difficulties. Since 1993 the school has run an exchange programme with partners in Frome's twin towns of Château Gontier (France) and Murrhardt (Germany). Each school takes turns to host annual multilateral visits, with 6–10 pupils from each school involved. As staying in host families would present too great a challenge for many pupils, alternative arrangements are made: pupils from all three countries are accommodated together staying in the school, in a local hostel or trust house.

The three schools worked together on a Comenius project (through the British Council) based on the environment. Critchill School is not in a very culturally diverse area, and it is evident that the project and the exchanges really broadened pupils' horizons. Communicating and mixing with pupils in other countries helped them to see cultural diversity as something to be celebrated and not feared. The students discuss what they have seen and describe their experiences in a very positive way. They have grown in confidence in handling relationships within a different cultural experience and their motivation in a range of subjects has improved.

(From 'Let's do something special...', *News: The Magazine of the Central Bureau*, Spring 2001)

A module focusing on a country

At Montacute School, each spring term, for the Upper School (Years 7–11 and post-16), a country is chosen from the geography National Curriculum framework, and much work that term is associated with that country – music, drama, art, food, language, religion, geography and history. The school feels that this approach gives all pupils a range of opportunities, including many sensory experiences. Pupils are encouraged to use the internet to explore relevant websites associated with the country – they can find out about food and customs, and play games on some websites. The finale to the term is a special 'country' afternoon. Countries previously chosen include France, Ireland, Mexico, Japan, India, Australia and Egypt.

Such cross-curricular projects have elements of many different subject areas within them. However, such activities can appropriately be given a strong citizenship emphasis.

The Save the Children resource pack (2002) adds to these ideas through the use of photos, pictures and maps, adapted here to be more accessible:

- Putting myself in the picture – blu-tack a picture of themselves onto a selected photo and try to imagine themselves in these new surroundings – what is around them, sights, sounds, smells, etc. Initially picture self in a range of familiar surroundings so there are concrete experiences to draw on.
- Cropping – photocopy or crop pictures in such a way to encourage them to imagine what lies 'outside' the picture/frame. Stick this onto a larger sheet and ask them to draw or add to the 'bigger picture'. Look for clues in the photo that might tell them about what they see.
- Talking time – ask them to select a photo by one criterion, e.g. which do they like best; which surprised them most; which would they like most to find out more about, and why, to each of these questions.
- Question time – what do they want to know for each picture? Use symbol cues for types of questions, e.g. about people, their jobs, homes, families, food.
- Journeys – use maps or atlases to get students to think about travel between destinations shown. Identify the different methods of travel, countries/places they would travel through, what geographical features would they see (rivers, mountains, sea)? What would the weather be like? What problems might they encounter? Initially, start with a map of a very familiar place – classroom, school, playground, then on to local area. Follow a route on your map – to the swimming pool, the local park. What features do you see on the journey?

- Making links – using an enlarged map find the countries linked to children in resource pack photos. Find connections with these places – where they were born; relatives live there; they holidayed there. Try to make broader connections that link with your local community – range of foods available in supermarkets, restaurants, twin towns. Make a visual display of these links.

What's for lunch?

This activity is linked through the 'Montage Plus' section of the British Council website (www.britishcouncil.org/education/schools/index.htm). The project looks at the different experiences of people around the world as they sit down to open their lunchboxes. Focusing on cultural diversity, healthy eating and a broadening of understanding, the project seeks to promote debate and exchange between students across the globe.

Production to consumption

Following a product from raw material to consumption can provide pupils with a wider global knowledge and understanding about interdependence. Fairtrade and Oxfam (www.fairtrade.org.uk; www.oxfam.org.uk) both produce useful resources; for example photographs and games about the production of chocolate, raising awareness that 99 per cent of people who grow cocoa beans have not seen chocolate and 99 per cent of people who eat chocolate have never seen a cocoa bean.

Countries on the meridian (http://www.oxfam.org.uk/coolplanet/ontheline/)

'On the Line' was a millennium project which celebrated the diversity of culture in the countries on the zero-degree meridian line. The website contains resources on environmental issues; virtual journeys, country by country; and online teaching materials.

Water (from IfC 2002: Global community; Water works)

Activities here support the development of understanding that clean water is a limited resource in many parts of the world. Pupils could carry water some distance; try and distinguish between clean and dirty water (not always possible visibly); measure how much water they use for different everyday activities. The WaterAid website (www.wateraid.org.uk) provides further ideas and information.

Story: Five Little Fiends, by Sarah Dyer

This is a story about the interdependence of elements of the environment. It tells the tale of five fiends who lived in statues on a large plain and each day came out to marvel at their surroundings. They decided to take home the thing they liked best, so one took the sun, one the land, one the sky, one the sea and one the moon. They kept them in their individual statues and admired them until they realised that each of the elements from their environment needed each other to exist meaningfully – for example, 'the sky was nowhere to be found without the land', so they returned them to their surroundings.

Local environmental issues

Tidying (developed from IfC 2002, The environment)

These resource materials include 'spot the difference' pictures of areas before and after tidying – a school cloakroom and a library area. These can be used for comparisons and discussion. Scenarios may be played out to consider the importance of tidiness. The above resources suggest:

- tripping over a shoe;
- a wheelchair cannot pass as there is too much rubbish in the way;
- you cannot find a teaspoon as someone has left it in the wrong place;
- rubbish smells bad and encourages rats;
- you cannot find your favourite book as the book corner is a mess.

Pupils could investigate their own school to locate areas which may need tidying and take their own 'before' and 'after' photographs. They may tidy up the classroom, their school bag, a resources box, the local playground or park. Staff may set up the classroom with many things in the wrong place and encourage students to identify 'What's wrong?' and put things in their correct places.

Rubbish rap

A class at Meldreth Manor participated in a rubbish rap with associated activities (Figure 5.5). This was based on a song 'Pollution' (Education through Music 1994). The class collected and made a huge mobile of assorted plastic bags for a Waste Aware Day. The rap was used for drumming, clapping, beating and music making.

Pollution!

Look at all our rubbish – it's all in
  Orchard Hall
We're into green recycling at Meldreth
  Manor School

Let's clean it up! (clap clap)
Let's clean it up! (clap clap)
And take more care.

Look at all our plastic bags, hanging
  all around
They may get thrown upon a tip or
  buried in the ground

Let's clean it up! (clap clap)
Let's clean it up! (clap clap)
And take more care.

The waste and all the rubbish that we
  all produce each day
It's not a danger to our health if safely
  put away

The minibus and all our cars, they
  make the car park stink
The smell and fumes and noise you
  hear, it really makes you think

All those bags and packets and cans of
  drink as well
We'll make the place look better – we
  hope that you can tell

Let's clean it up! (clap clap)
Let's clean it up! (clap clap)
And take more care

And take more care

And take more care

And take more care (fading away)

Class 12
8 March 2002

Figure 5.5 Meldreth Manor School: Rubbish Rap (based on the song 'Pollution', Education through Music 1994)

Eco-schools Awards (www.eco-schools.org)

In 1999/2000 Montacute School focused on the environment for their Eco-schools silver award. Their aims as a school for this challenge were:

- to become more aware of global and local environmental issues;
- to become more involved in community decision-making;
- to become more aware of energy and water usage and conservation.

They set a range of targets for the year. These are reproduced in Figure 5.6.

Montacute School – Targets for 'The Environment' 1999–2000

Help us become an 'Eco-friendly' School.

Our aims are to become more aware of global and local environmental issues; to become involved in community decision-making; to become more aware of energy and water usage and conservation.

AT MONTACUTE SCHOOL WE WILL:

- Send out PLANET PLEDGE leaflets to parents.
- Participate in the ECO-SCHOOLS AWARD.
- Design an ECO-CODE for the school.
- Have a Whole-School ENVIRONMENTAL AWARENESS WEEK.
- Join 'ROOTS AND SHOOTS'.
- Listen to the views of our children.
- Collect ALUMINIUM FOIL for LODGE HILL.
- Design 'Switch-Off' light symbols to go above light switches.
- Collect PRINTER-INK CARTRIDGES for W.W.F.
- Lower School will participate in a WATER PROJECT.
- Leavers and Senior 3, will help with WOODLAND MANAGEMENT, PLANTING AROUND SCHOOL, MAKE BAT-BOXES, CLEAN OUT BIRD BOXES, PROVIDE WORMS FOR WORMERY, MAKE BIRD-PUDDINGS FOR BIRD-TABLES.
- Kann-Do It Enterprise make and sell BIRD-PUDDINGS and bags of BIRD-FOOD. Make cards from RECYCLED PAPER.
- Buy a SHREDDER and sell shredded-paper for pet bedding.
- Visit the EARTHKIND ship at Poole Quay.
- Visit the ORGANIC GARDEN at OAKDALE.
- Complete the first phase of OUR SCHOOL GROUNDS PROJECT.
- Encourage a greater awareness of school TIDINESS and SAFETY. Staff and Classes to be responsible for different areas of the school.
- Care for CLASS PLANTS

Figure 5.6 Montacute School: Eco-school targets

Recycling projects (from IfC 2002, The environment)

Students can sort rubbish into different categories – reusable, waste and objects to be tidied and put in their correct places. They can then sort the waste items into paper, glass, organic and plastic. Students can explore ways of reusing materials, e.g. making models and musical instruments or reducing waste materials.

The website http://www.childrenoftheearth.org has a 'Cool Multimedia' section which includes a multimedia presentation on recycling.

Low-impact packed lunch

Pupils can look at different packed lunches and consider the amount and type of waste. They can design a low-impact packed lunch, perhaps as a competition, with minimal waste or waste only for composting or reuse.

Political literacy/government and democracy

Accessing political literacy for pupils with learning difficulties means helping pupils to be politically aware and effective. It is partly concerned with knowledge about political and economic systems, but it is also about participation and decision-making and having a say. We have already emphasised the importance of staff in promoting this way of working and providing appropriate concrete and real opportunities.

School councils are one way of enabling participation in the decision-making processes of a school. Chapter 6 relates entirely to school councils and the issues and implications for pupils with learning difficulties.

Decision-making

Examples of how these might arise in 'real life' school contexts are given in *Planning, Teaching and Assessing the Curriculum for Pupils with Learning Difficulties: PSHE and Citizenship* for Key Stage 3:

> As part of their regular classroom and school routines at Key Stage 3, pupils participate, negotiate and make real choices and informed decisions. They may:
>
> - make decisions about individual and group activities;
> - give permission and withhold their permission – for example about personal space or intimate care procedures;
> - choose future curriculum options;
> - explore their choice of break-time activities and agree to have different activities available on different days;
> - decide what to sell in the school tuck shop after considering healthy eating options, or carry out a survey and find out what other pupils prefer;
> - elect pupils and make decision as part of a school council;
> - identify issues in the school and suggest solutions and improvements.
>
> (QCA 2001c: 21)

Topical issues: questions to ask (Hicks 2001)

In order to make informed decisions or to be aware of how their decisions are influenced, activities centred around topical issues can be useful. These can stem from current news or school events, but will often need direction to lead pupils through the processes.

i) What is the issue?

What do we think, feel, hope and fear, in relation to this particular issue? What do others who are involved think, feel and say?

ii) How has it come about?

Why do we and others think, feel and act in the way we do? What and who have influenced us and others involved? What is the history of this situation?

iii) Who gains, who loses?

Who has the power in this situation and how do they use it? Is it used to the advantage of some and the disadvantage of others? If so, in what way?

iv) What is our vision?

What would things look like in a more just, peaceful and sustainable future, for ourselves and others? What values will we use to guide our choices?

v) What can be done?

What are the possible courses of action open to us? What are others already doing? Which course of action is most likely to achieve our vision of a preferred future?

vi) How will we do it?

How shall we implement our plan of action in school, at home, or in the community? How shall we work together? Whose help might we need? How do we measure our success?

Debate

The forum for more formal debate was discussed in the previous chapter, as one means of preparing for decision-making. This is also an approach that fits well to model practice in government procedures. Gregory (2002) provides the suggested running order of a debate:

- The chairperson welcomes the speakers and the audience.
- First speaker from Side A delivers his/her speech.
- First speaker from Side B delivers his/her speech.
- Second speaker from Side A delivers his/her speech.
- Second speaker from Side B delivers his/her speech.
- First speaker from Side A sums up in one sentence.
- First speaker from Side B sums up in one sentence.
- Finally, the chairperson takes the vote and then announces who is the winner of the debate.

Other opportunities can be devised using interactive stories with decision points that allow flexibility in how the story progresses. The whole class has to decide what to do next. How shall we decide?

Laws

Starting points may be the more obvious and accessible laws – for example rules for traffic lights, speeding, thieving.

Visit from local community police officers may enable pupils to become more aware of the role of the police in upholding the law. For example, they may demonstrate uniform and equipment, discuss laws relating to different ages, alert pupils to dangers, inspire role-play activity. Laws can connect to the safeguarding of rights.

Government

Local government (from QCA 2001c: 24)

Pupils can investigate the role of local government. They may find out what local government does, for example, and meet and interview members of the council, their MP or the mayor/mayoress. They may carry out surveys on people's opinions on particular issues in the school or community, and record and present their findings. They may visit the local council chamber and, perhaps, hold a meeting there or attend a council meeting.

Voting and elections

Different ways of voting (from IfC 2002, Government)

This activity uses a real situation and trials different ways of voting and coming to a decision.

Explain that there will be a small party today but the class will have to decide and agree what they will all eat and drink and the music they will listen to:

- Names in a hat:
  Show the class a choice of three CDs and explain that the pupil whose name is pulled out of a hat will decide which CD they will listen to. Each pupil should be given a piece of paper with their name written on it to put into the hat, so that they all know that their names have been included before one is picked out. Is the class happy with this? Is it a fair way to decide? How else could they have chosen?
- Show of hands:
  Show the class a choice of three different drinks and ask them to decide which they would like to drink by a show of hands. The teacher should record the names of the pupils who vote for each drink, to reinforce the idea that everyone knows who voted for which drink.
- Ballot paper:
  Show the class a choice of three different types of food and a ballot paper and explain that they will decide in secret which they would like to eat. Explain that the papers will be counted after everyone has voted and that they will eat the food that has the most votes. Count the votes in a way that is visual, perhaps by putting the appropriate number of balls next to each item to represent how many pupils voted for it.

The vote will be more realistic if there are some campaigns beforehand so that pupils feel uncomfortable about voting for crisps in front of the pupil who was campaigning for chocolate and thus come to appreciate the advantages of a secret ballot.

(Institute for Citizenship 2002, Government: 5)

Hold your own elections

There are a number of points for consideration in holding a mock election, many of which can be discussed with pupils. For example:

- What is the rationale for the event?
- Real or imaginary parties? (if held at a local or national election time)
- What kinds of issues?
- What will be involved in the election processes?
- What will be involved on polling day? What voting procedures?
- How will candidates be chosen? (e.g. being proposed by a classmate, supported by two other pupils and producing a 'manifesto')
- How will campaign teams be chosen? What activities will they engage in?
- Advertising posters? Leaflets? Meetings? Addressing assembly? Mock radio/TV broadcast?
- How will results be presented and discussed?

(adapted from Davies 1996)

Economy

Pupils learn about banking and the economy in meaningful ways. They may practise managing money in a range of situations; they may experience a variety of transactions and exchanges – for example, they may run a token economy trading system.

This is an example from *Planning, Teaching and Assessing the Curriculum for Pupils with Learning Difficulties: PSHE and Citizenship* for Key Stage 4:

Pupils have opportunities to learn about and experience some financial services and economic functions. They may:

- have work experience in running the school bank – for example, they count money, fill in and stamp books and deal with customers;
- use a bank to save money, visit local banks and explore some of the work carried out there;
- plan, budget, spend and keep accounts in a mini-enterprise scheme.

(QCA 2001c: 24–5)

Mini-enterprise

Mini-enterprise activities are useful in involving pupils in decision-making processes, in a concrete and real situation, which can mimic business enterprise. Indeed, business links can form part of the procedures. Mini-enterprise can include formal structures with pupils taking the roles of chairperson, financial adviser, company secretary, production manager, advertising manager, etc. The Team Enterprise scheme (for young people with learning difficulties) involves setting up a company, selling shares in the company, attending trade fairs and exhibitions with other schools.

Team Enterprise is part of Young Enterprise (www.young-enterprise.org.uk).

Media

Making the news

A meaningful activity is for students to 'make' their own news. They may use personal and local news about themselves, the school and the immediate community. They may interview people, and tape-record or video the interviews. They may take photographs or draw an artist's impression. They can then present the news as a display, newspaper or TV news bulletin. They may contribute to local news – for example writing a letter to the local newspaper.

What's in the news? (from QCA 2001c)

Pupils can examine sources of news information locally and globally – for example, internet, local and national newspapers, TV and radio. They explore how the media presents information and how it affects opinions.

Current affairs discussions and debates

It could be a daily activity for students to look at current or topical issues – sport, fashion, pop, politics. At the end of the week, they may choose an issue based on agreed criteria (most interesting, popular, controversial) and vote. There is a role for a clerk.

Advertising (from IfC 2002, Media)

Pupils may investigate adverts and identify the item advertised. They may consider a number of questions:

- What is the advert for? Communicate what the product is. Sample the product.
- Who is the advert aimed at? (children, teenagers, or adults)
- Do we have that item at home or in school?
- Do we like that product personally?
- How does the advert make us feel?
- Does the advert tell a story?
- Does the advert use words, music, colours or anything else to make us feel like that?
- Has watching the advert made us feel differently about the product?

(Institute for Citizenship 2002 Media: 5)

Pupils could make their own video advert, participating in a range of decisions – for example choosing the product, deciding upon music and/or words, deciding upon the story to tell. They may play different roles – for example, acting, singing, operating a tape-recorder/CD-player, camera operator, editor.

They could make a fake advert deliberately intended to deceive. For example, 'Buy these shoes made from paper – perfect to use in the rain.'

Public services

Again, an example is provided in *Planning, Teaching and Assessing the Curriculum for Pupils with Learning Difficulties: PSHE and Citizenship* for Key Stage 4.

> Pupils explore and investigate public services and leisure facilities in the local community. They may:
>
> - visit the local swimming pool and meet the people who help run it;
> - explore the range of leisure facilities in the community, by obtaining information from a local newspaper and telephone directories;
> - take part in community activities, evaluate 'value for money' and use this information to make choices and decisions about the use of their leisure time.
>
> (QCA 2001c: 24)

CHAPTER SIX

School councils

Introduction

School councils can create an invaluable forum through which a real voice and real power can meaningfully be devolved to young people. When valued, their opinions and decisions can make a genuine difference. School councils, once well established, can be involved at an influential level within school decision-making processes and actually facilitate school-wide change.

As Taylor (2002) notes, a school council can have different aims; it may help pupils better understand democratic procedures to become participative members of society in the future; to respect children's rights; to promote better behaviours; or to provide opportunities for service. The distinctions are important as they raise questions about underlying philosophy and principle – for example, is there a philosophy of empowerment?

These councils need to be involved in real decisions and to move beyond a forum for student criticism, as Ruddock *et al.* (1997) describe, 'an exercise in damage limitation rather than an opportunity for constructive consultation'. Discussions about uniform, toilets and lunchtime clubs are important, but school councils need to move beyond this to participate in major decision-making processes.

How can we do this with meaning and success for pupils with learning difficulties?

Some examples:

- Owen and Tarr (1998) examine the setting up of a school council in a special school for children with moderate learning difficulties, physical disabilities and emotional and behavioural difficulties. The school council made a substantial impact on improving the physical environment of the school, collecting evidence through video data about the school environment and the views of children, and approaching the governors.
- At Sunfield School, some school councillors meet with, and are consulted about, interviewees for staff appointments.
- One school commented to us, 'The school council has been in operation for one year and has proved to be an excellent forum for making things happen and pupils making choices, being more responsible and learning they can change things.' (Montacute School)

Benefits and principles

In the context of primary schools, Rowe (2001: 44–5) lists the benefits to children from involvement in a school council:

- a better understanding of their problems;
- a say in matters which concern them;
- opportunities to learn about the way organisations function, including how resources are deployed and shared problems are addressed;
- increased self-confidence in tackling issues, being proactive, speaking in public, debating issues and handling matters in a business-like manner;
- opportunities to become more socially and morally responsible;
- a greater sense of community across all the school years;
- a practical chance to plan for change and see the benefits in reality; and
- increased self-esteem.

He also identifies benefits to the school:

- greater awareness of pupil issues and of the realities of the school experience;
- greater pupil involvement in school affairs as pupils assist in the implementation of school policy;
- harnessing of pupil energy and enthusiasm, such as in fundraising and organising events;
- increased pupil responsibility and ownership of the school, including the grounds and shared property;
- school policies that are better grounded in pupil realities; and
- established consultation procedures to facilitate good and efficient decision-making.

Davies (1999), in her research, highlighted ways in which school councils can help reduce exclusions. The principles emerging from this project include:

- giving pupils a 'voice' and encouraging skills of self-advocacy;
- giving pupils a sense of 'agency', of their role in achieving change;
- giving pupils practice in decision-making and choice, both in curriculum and behaviour;
- maximum equity between staff and pupils, with pupils treated with the same respect as adults; and
- inclusion for all, with achievable targets and visible success.

Although this project was centred on mainstream schools, these very principles reflect the needs of all pupils and are particularly relevant and significant for pupils with learning difficulties.

The remainder of this chapter considers different points and issues in establishing and running school councils, with reference to pupils with learning difficulties:

- getting support
- structure of the council
- the election process
- frequency, timing and place of meetings
- the chair
- link teacher/adviser
- process of meetings
- issues for a school council
- case studies
- guidelines for practice

Getting support

Staff, governors and parents

Taylor (2002) suggests that the ethos and culture of a school will affect how easy it is to set up a school council. To be most effective, Winup (1994) purports, the setting up of a committee or council must 'be embedded in a whole-school approach to the area of self-advocacy'.

Staff need to agree with the role, value and status of a school council. A link person will probably be required to support the council. By involving parents and governors in this initiative, too, schools are highlighting the value placed upon pupil involvement, providing a role model of respect and clarifying the school ethos in practice.

Pupils

Pupils need to understand the role and purpose of a school council. This may involve much preparatory work. Montacute School held a meeting with upper school students to discuss possibilities (see Figure 6.1). They also watched videos of how other schools operate their school councils/voting procedures.

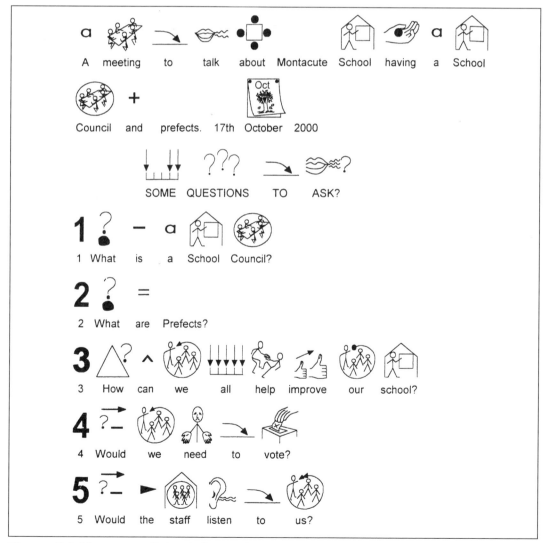

Figure 6.1 Montacute School: A meeting to talk about setting up a school council

Sunfield School have a School Council notice-board which includes names and photographs of all the council members and information about 'Democracy in Action'. This explains the role of the student council, how you can become a member of the student council, and indicates some of the things a councillor could be asked to do as part of his/her important role. A small part of this is shown in Figure 6.2.

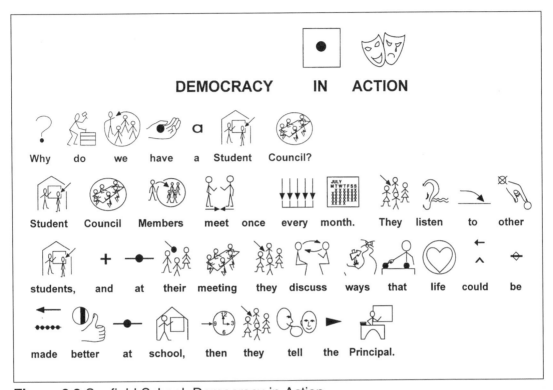

Figure 6.2 Sunfield School: Democracy in Action

School Councils UK recommend setting up a working party, which includes pupils, to be responsible for preparing for the school council. This may involve publicity – for example poster countdowns to election day, and preparations for elections.

Structure of the council

What is the best make up for the council?

Some school councils include only pupils; others include representatives from the different staffing groups in the school – for example, a representative from the cleaning staff, midday supervisory assistants, administrative staff, teaching assistants, governors and a teacher, in addition to pupils. Some involve senior staff to signal the significance of the proceedings.

Rowe (2001) argues that 'adults should not be seen or felt to dominate the school council. However, it is important to involve adults other than the teaching staff.'

There are a number of questions to resolve:

- How many pupils (e.g. two from each class)? At Piper Hill School in Manchester (Otten 1999) one pupil is elected from each tutor group to be a representative.

- What about gender balance: should each class elect a boy and a girl?
- What age groups? Rowe (2001: 45) maintains, 'It seems better to assume that all age groups should be represented.'
- How can you ensure representation of all abilities in the school? How can pupils with profound and multiple learning difficulties be enabled to participate? How representative are the pupil councillors?
- What should the term of office be – one term, one year? One term extends the opportunities for more pupils to be involved, but is not perhaps long enough for pupils with learning difficulties to gain full understanding of the procedures.
- Should pupils be allowed to stand for election again? Should all pupils have the opportunity to represent their class?

Underlying structures

Davies (1999: 3) points out 'the need for a supporting structure of class, year or tutor group councils, or circle time, to involve all pupils in the school'. School Councils UK recommend circle time as a basis for pupil councils. They suggest that through circle time, children learn to:

- speak in turn
- listen to others
- respect other people's opinions which are different from their own
- express their own views. (Clay, 2000: 21)

They also suggest class councils for discussing class issues, for receiving information back from the school council, for raising issues to take to the school council and for helping all students to learn skills and develop confidence to participate in the school council activities. Gold and Gold (1998) point out that classroom councils are based on the classroom as a mini-community which is part of the larger community of the school.

Structures need to go the other way too, fitting in with wider decision-making bodies in the school so that, for example, minutes of the school council meetings are fed into staff, senior management and governors meetings.

The election process

There needs to be preparation, a programme of awareness, for the process of elections. This may involve practice meetings (see 'Process of meetings' below) in order for students to gauge some understanding of what happens in meetings and what it might entail to be a school council member. Students might consider the qualities needed to be a council member. Those who wish to stand for, or are nominated for, election could create a manifesto to inform voters of their qualities and attributes: for example, this could be in the form of a speech, poster, video or PowerPoint presentation, with peer support as appropriate. Election material can be displayed around school and hustings held.

Processes of voting could replicate those of a local or national parliamentary election with a secret ballot box and ballot papers – these could include photographs of the pupils standing for election. Different roles could be performed by pupils – for example, vote counters or returning officer – and the results could be announced formally in assembly.

It is useful to hold school council elections to coincide with local council elections, thus using the school council elections as an opportunity to learn about wider elections, different systems of voting and the role of a representative.

Frequency, timing and place of meetings

The timing and place of the meetings gives messages about value – for example, if they are only held during lunchtimes or break-times they may be construed as having little value.

Too many meetings, Rowe (2001) suggests, can cause fatigue and a sense of time-wasting; too few, alternatively, can fail to create a sense of involvement and momentum for the pupils. In Davies' (1999: 24) research of school councils in primary, secondary and special schools, she found that

> in schools where the council met only once every half term, it was not seen by pupils as so effective as those where it met once a month or a fortnight, or where it was supported by more regular year group or circle time meetings.

Thus, meetings need to be regular, perhaps every 2–4 weeks. Winup's committee met weekly for 20 minutes.

Some schools hold their school council meetings in the staffroom with refreshments provided. Kingsley School, use the head teacher's office for meetings. Both of these lend a sense of importance to the occasion.

The chair

Who chairs the council?

Clough and Holden (2002) suggest this role is carried out by someone with status, for example, the head teacher, a governor or the head girl or boy.

Cunningham (2000) disagrees, arguing that the head should not be too closely associated with the school council. We agree, and believe the role should be carried out by one of the pupils. However, it is likely that school councils in schools for children with learning difficulties may need the support of an adult to facilitate and enable. As Owen and Tarr (1998: 88) found:

> In mainstream school councils, pupil autonomy is of primary importance with adults attending only when specifically invited. In the context of a special school for young people with learning disabilities, some support from staff was needed to develop levels of personal autonomy.

For how long should the chair's position be held? In some schools the role is rotated each meeting (for example, at Kingsley School), or each half-term, around the members of the school council.

Winup's (1994) student committee defined the role of the chairperson as:

- to open a meeting;
- to make sure that each member who wants to speak is given an opportunity to do so;
- to make sure one person speaks at a time;
- to keep members to the point being discussed;
- to make a decision by calling a vote;
- to end the meeting. (p. 108)

Winup also includes the definitions of secretary (to write the agenda for meetings; to write up the minutes; to recall the minutes at each meeting) and treasurer (to keep account of all monies; to open and look after a bank account).

Link teacher/adviser

Rowe (2001: 45), in the context of school councils in primary settings, talks about a 'link teacher'. He describes the role of this job as to:

- act as mentor and trainer to the children;
- give advice and information but not dictate the council's decisions;
- assist the children between meetings to carry out any designated tasks and to prepare for the next meeting;
- act as a close link with the head, who may or may not attend all council meetings;
- act as a point of reference for other staff on council matters, encouraging good feedback to the whole school.

Winup (1994: 108) describes the role of adviser to the student committee thus:

- to become a guide at meetings and not a leader;
- to give assistance and advice when the group needs it;
- to teach the skills of the offices and committee procedure;
- to encourage ideas of the committee which could lead into action.

Taylor's (2002) recent research on school councils in primary and secondary schools in the UK found that there was 'usually a good deal of teacher intervention', despite teachers stating they played a minimal facilitating role.

The role of a link teacher or adviser is especially significant, but complex, for pupils with learning difficulties. They may need a greater level of support and facilitation in order to participate effectively, yet the council proceedings, discussions and decisions should be led by students.

Process of meetings

Participation

Pupils may need to be taught skills for participation.

The processes of formal meetings can be practised in classes. The Institute for Citizenship resource materials (2002: 4) suggest a discussion on favourite foods (using a simple focus for discussion may enable concentration on the processes of the meeting).

> The chair practises introducing the discussion and arranges whose turn it is to speak.
>
> The chair asks each person in turn to take the 'speaking object' and tell the group what their favourite food is. The secretary places a photo of the speaker onto the agenda sheet, followed by the appropriate symbol to record what the speaker said. These are the 'minutes'.
>
> After the meeting, the secretary reads the 'minutes' of the meeting, with help from staff where needed.
>
> Pupils and staff agree or disagree that the minutes are a true representation of the discussion.
>
> Other pupils can be chosen as chair and secretary to discuss the other topics.

Pupils may also practise and concentrate on relevant skills for participation in meetings, for example, active listening, communicating, taking turns, representation of others' views. Symbol prompts for some of these skills could be used as reminders during meetings.

At Kingsley School some of the children on the school council are responsible for ensuring that everyone's 'voice is heard' and work towards enabling the children with more profound needs who are also on the council to have auditory/object or visual choices and to recognising their responses.

Communication

Clough and Holden (2002) include this issue in terms of school councillors having the time and forum to communicate with the group of students they represent – for example through circle-time sessions or PSHE lessons; through the keeping of minutes; and using the school council notice-board.

These points are important for pupils with learning difficulties too. Communication in this context, however, has a different meaning in terms of how meaningful communication can be facilitated and how all modes of communication are recognised and valued through school council processes.

Minutes

Minutes can be recorded in symbolic form. They should be made widely available and, as a matter of course, disseminated to all pupils.

At Kingsley School the head teacher takes the minutes, which are then typed up by, and distributed by, pupils. At some schools the school bursar takes the minutes, again lending the task a sense of importance.

Figure 6.3 shows part of a set of school council minutes for the school council of Lakeside School. Items 2 and 4 (not shown) were about the election of chair, and a lengthy discussion about lunchtime clubs and playtimes. This included a problem of pupils running through the ball skills court and onto the infants playground, and a suggested solution of using a chain to keep the gate closed.

Agenda

Meldreth Manor School uses a standing agenda (Figure 6.4). These are laminated and small lumps of blu-tack are used to indicate the stage of the meeting on the agenda.

Figure 6.5 shows an agenda from Montacute School produced by a School Councillor after finding out from classes items for discussion.

Rituals and routines

It is important for many pupils with learning difficulties that elements of routine and ritual are built into school council proceedings, to act as reminders and cues. In formalising meetings, schools may use robes or hats to signify the 'move' into a meeting, use the same room, follow the same standing agenda and use a special 'speaking' object to pass round for each pupil to make their contribution in turn.

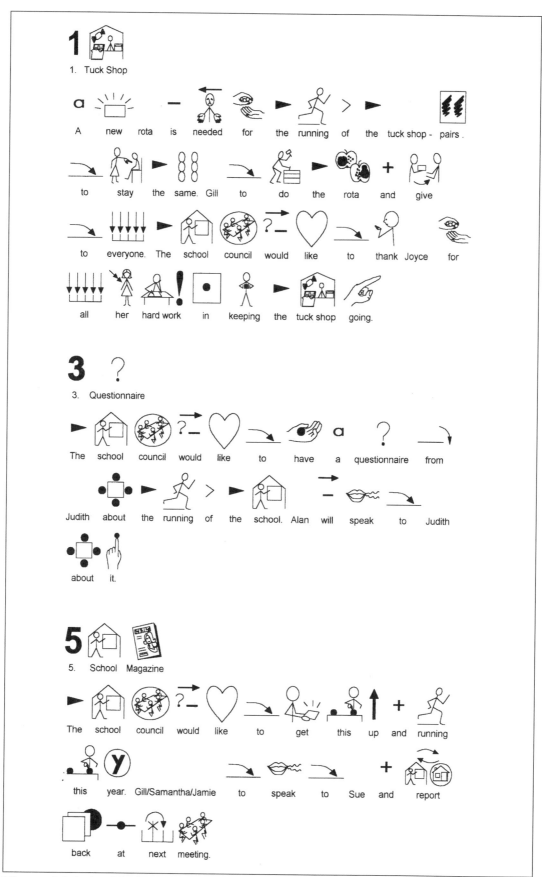

1. Tuck Shop

A new rota is needed for the running of the tuck shop - pairs . to stay the same. Gill to do the rota and give to everyone. The school council would like to thank Joyce for all her hard work in keeping the tuck shop going.

3. Questionnaire

The school council would like to have a questionnaire from Judith about the running of the school. Alan will speak to Judith about it.

5. School Magazine

The school council would like to get this up and running this year. Gill/Samantha/Jamie to speak to Sue and report back at next meeting.

Figure 6.3 Lakeside School: School Council minutes

School Council <u>Agenda</u> Date:

1. Welcome

2. Notes

3. Items to discuss

4. Action

Figure 6.4 Meldreth Manor School: School Council Standing Agenda

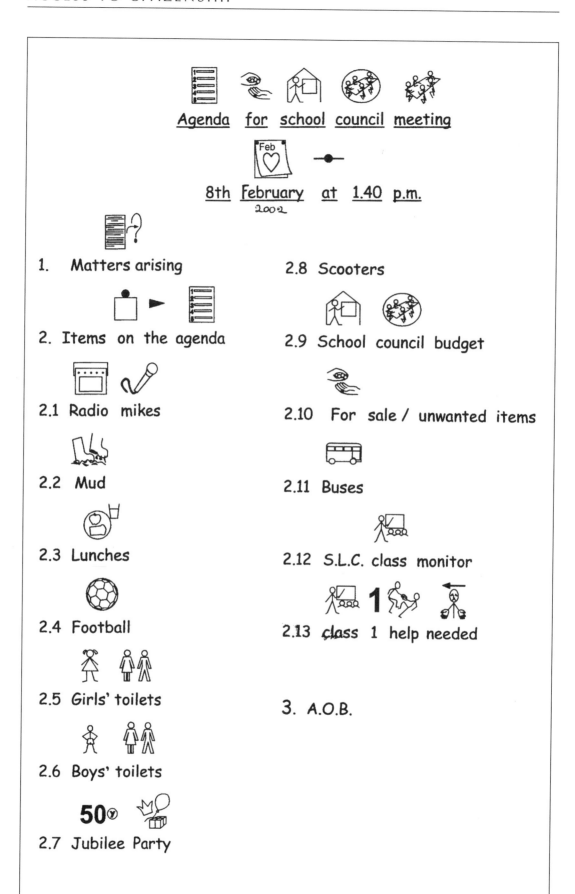

Figure 6.5 Montacute School: Agenda for School Council meeting

Issues for a school council

These may come from the pupils – for example from class councils or circle time. They may also come to the council from other meetings, including staff, senior management and governors' meetings. Discussions may take on a different dimension if the school council is allocated its own budget.

A suggestion from the Institute for Citizenship resource materials (2002) is a survey of pupils' thoughts and feelings about the school to provide starting points for the school councils. School council members may ask pupils for their views, act as peer advocates through close knowledge of others or use a written or symbol-based questionnaire. For example, they could ask whether pupils like school, what they like best and what makes them happy/sad at school. They could focus on different aspects of school life – friendships, school dinners, break-times, uniform, curriculum.

The issues for discussion are often pertinent to the pupils' lives and 'affect the quality of the children's lives in school' (Davies 1996: 124). The work of the council can thus have genuine relevance. Winup's (1994) student committee, for instance, achieved, in its first year, the introduction of lunchtime activities, a rota for the snooker table and computers, the holding of sponsored events to raise money, the purchase of new equipment for the common-room and the opening and running of a tuck shop.

At Kingsley School the school council has selected names for the class groups, first agreeing name themes for each part of the school. Thus Key Stage 1 classes are themed as fruit and are called 'apples' and 'bananas'; lower Key Stage 2 are named after wild animals and upper Key Stage 2 as birds. The school council has decided the decoration and colours for the school entrance hall and the music to be played in the entrance hall to signify entering and leaving school each day. In addition, they have decided on use of areas of the playground, developments in the sensory garden and their own Christmas special events.

It is important, however, to also include issues that relate specifically to teaching and learning. For example, consulting pupils on new school policies and curriculum changes. Sunfield School Council, for example, made a response to the DfES for the consultation on the Green Paper *14–19 Extending Opportunities, Raising Standards*. They were informed by their link member of staff that the government wished to know what students aged 14–19 wanted to learn in school. They commented that they wanted more work skills and work experience and to be more like the 16–19 department in the school. These comments were sent on their behalf as part of the consultation.

The Institute for Citizenship resources (2002) include the following suggestions as starter ideas for school councils:

Physical environment

- Colour of walls, doors and carpets for different areas of school
- Notice boards in the entrance hall
- Areas of school to be decorated and in which order
- Front door of school
- Areas of planting in borders or tubs around school, e.g. small sensory garden area
- Playground markings
- Position of benches or picnic tables in the play areas

Playtimes

- 'Buddy system' at playtimes
- Playground equipment or games
- Lunchtime clubs

Uniform

- Introduction of school uniform within school
- Choice of style and colour of uniform

Lunchtime

- Trays or plates/plastic or disposable cups?
- Changes to menu if practical
- Music at lunchtime – what kind of music?

Educational visits

- Where each group should go as an end of term visit or treat
- What colour the school minibus should be (if practical)
- Pupils can vote on what their school mascot is and what it is called

Reward systems

- Prizes for pupils with most 'reward points'
- Where to situate 'star of the week' photographs
- What colour certificates should be for each Key Stage
- Nominate pupils for 'endeavour' awards

Community

- Does the school want to raise money for a charity? Which one?
- Fundraising events within school
- Helping a community group with fundraising
- Recycle or litter picking schemes
- Helping other groups within school

Whole school issues

- Commenting on policies
- Involvement in Healthy Schools Standard
- School Council budget

(Institute for Citizenship 2002 School Councils: 9–10)

Case studies

Montacute School Council

The idea of having a School Council came from senior pupils in an RE session. Our first meeting was held in January 2001 and the Officers were elected. We have Class Monitors who represent pupils in the early years and the Supported Learning Class.

Our aim is to make Montacute an excellent school and the student School Councillors responsible members of the school. The Council Meetings provide a forum for sharing ideas, making decisions and listening to each other.

This is what we have achieved since January 2001:

- We have 4 prefects and 9 Class Monitors.
- A privacy screen has been erected in the Boys' Toilets.
- A Maths Fair was organised in aid of UNICEF – £124 raised.
- A lunchtime Animal Club has started.
- A litter-bin purchased for the playground.
- A leisure area has been improved and new outdoor games and bikes bought.
- Senior swimming kits are sent home each week.
- A Road Safety Week was organised.
- Post-16 group collect waste paper for recycling.
- The corridor is tidier.

November 2001   Compiled for School Council Notice Board

Meldreth Manor School Council

Meldreth Manor is a SCOPE residential school and college offering residential and day education to pupils with profound and multiple learning difficulties. The school has a pre-16 and a 16+ department, whilst the college caters for 19+ students. The school was validated as a Health Promoting School in May 2000 and continues to strengthen its capacity as a healthy setting for living, learning and working.

The work of the School Council is still developing – when we set up the council we approached it as a joint venture, staff and pupils learning together. We have moved a fair way but there are still challenges to overcome.

Meldreth elected its first School Council in Autumn 2002, although some pupils already had some experience of representation through the lower school council which came into being during the previous year.

It was decided, however, that a council representative of the whole school was the preferred model. Discussion at the time as to whether or not the college should be represented resulted in a decision that they should not, and they have since evolved their own mechanisms for making their views felt.

Classes were invited to work through the election procedures over a period of two weeks' tutorial time. The meeting schedule is a fortnightly meeting on Wednesdays, 9.30–10.30 am.

Elections over, the council met together for the first time. We felt it was important to introduce a 'ritual', or regular procedure, to add significance and identity to the proceedings. (We are also thinking about introducing a piece of music or theme tune which will, over time, become associated with the council.) As pupils gather for the school council meeting they are given a yellow sash to denote membership and a large photo of each member goes up on the wall. We work to an agenda that is simple and accessible.

The meeting begins with a 'welcome' when members are encouraged to greet each other. We then recall the 'notes' from the previous meeting. This is the record we made at that meeting using a flip chart and rebus. The next item is 'items to discuss' – it might be feedback from classes or reporting back by staff on issues that have been raised. The last item on the agenda is 'action ' – the work that has to take place before we meet again.

We try to keep everyone in the school informed and aware of the council's work through the school newsletter and a dedicated school council notice-board. There are posters in every classroom and residential flat with names and photographs of members, and a mobile 'interactive' notice-board where pupils can listen to information about the council and leave a message if they wish. We have sent regular reports to the Governors.

The school council successfully applied to the Friends of Meldreth who made a grant to the council to use for out-of-school activities. The council has voted to hold an end-of-term picnic for all pupils and students to celebrate the end of a successful first year. It's a great way of celebrating and publicising the work of the council and an opportunity to hold an awards ceremony to thank this year's members for all their hard work.

Guidelines for practice

As a result of her survey and case study research on school councils in primary and secondary schools, Taylor (2002) suggests a number of guidelines for practice. Some of these are summarised below:

The council must be given a prominent status

- Display photographs of members.
- Give representatives badges.
- Provide a school council notice-board.
- Have a school council budget.
- Mention the school council in assemblies and newsletter.
- Allocate class time for feedback and discussion.
- Someone from the senior management team must be actively involved in supporting the council.
- Ensure staff are aware of decisions made during council meetings.
- Encourage involvement of governors.

Meetings and organisation

- Optimum frequency, timing and length of meetings needs deciding.
- Find a balance between giving as many children as possible a chance to be councillors, but giving them long enough to gain sufficient experience.

Councillors

- Preparation is valuable.
- Encourage an ethos where being a councillor is a 'respected and sought-after role'.

Non-councillors

- Give all students the opportunity to make suggestions.
- Ensure feedback to classes.
- Make sure each classroom has an ongoing record of council decisions.
- Attribute ideas which are followed up to their originators.

(summarised from Taylor 2002: 121–5)

Concluding comments

The focus of ideas in this book has been on interpreting citizenship education for young people with learning difficulties – what is most important is not the learning *about* citizenship, but the learning *through* citizenship and the implications this has for the way we work with, and relate to, pupils. We have the responsibility to make their learning more accessible and more meaningful, encouraging and enabling them to take a more active part. It is only by embedding this into the ethos, principles and practice in schools that we can strive to 'live and breathe' PSHE and citizenship, rather than merely teach it.

Ofsted (2002), already reports that the introduction of citizenship in schools has, in many secondary schools, led to subject departments reviewing their provision. Even if they do not make an explicit contribution to citizenship, it has caused departments to consider fundamentals such as how children learn, attitudes and opportunities to contribute to lessons. It is these fundamental principles that practitioners are encouraged to revisit.

Hopefully, in involving our current school population in active citizenship, we will be 'preparing the next generation of young people to work for and live in a more inclusive society' (Mittler 2000: 103). Benefits will perpetuate if citizens of the future have a better understanding of, and respect for, diversity, human rights and social justice.

The principles for citizenship we have emphasised echo and reinforce messages about inclusion. Citizenship education endorses and enhances inclusive practices and there is a powerful interdependency between effective citizenship and successful inclusion.

Appendix: National Curriculum PSHE and Citizenship framework

Key Stage 1 PSHE and Citizenship

1. Developing confidence and responsibility and making the most of their abilities

a) to recognise what they like and dislike, what is fair and unfair, and what is right and wrong	
b) to share their opinions on things that matter to them and explain their views	
c) to recognise, name and deal with their feelings in a positive way	
d) to think about themselves, learn from their experiences and recognise what they are good at	
e) how to set simple goals	

2. Preparing to play an active role as citizens

a) to take part in discussions with one other person and the whole class	
b) to take part in a simple debate about topical issues	
c) to recognise choices they can make, and recognise the difference between right and wrong	
d) to agree and follow rules for their group and classroom, and understand how rules help them	
e) to realise that people and other living things have needs, and that they have responsibilities to meet them	
f) that they belong to various groups and communities, such as family and school	

g) what improves and harms their local, natural and built environments and about some of the ways people look after them	
h) to contribute to the life of the class and school	
i) to realise that money comes from different sources and can be used for different purposes	

3. Developing a healthy, safer lifestyle

a) how to make simple choices that improve their health and well-being	
b) to maintain personal hygiene	
c) how some diseases spread and can be controlled	
d) about the process of growing from young to old and how people's needs change	
e) the names of the main parts of the body	
f) that all household products, including medicines, can be harmful if not used properly	
g) rules for, and ways of, keeping safe, including basic road safety, and about people who can help them to stay safe	

4. Developing good relationships and respecting the differences between people

a) to recognise how their behaviour affects other people	
b) to listen to other people, and play and work cooperatively	
c) to identify and respect the differences and similarities between people	
d) that family and friends should care for each other	
e) that there are different types of teasing and bullying, that bullying is wrong, and how to get help to deal with bullying	

Key Stage 2 PSHE and Citizenship

1. Developing confidence and responsibility and making the most of their abilities

a) to talk and write about their opinions, and explain their views, on issues that affect themselves and society	
b) to recognise their worth as individuals by identifying positive things about themselves and their achievements, seeing their mistakes, making amends and setting personal goals	
c) to face new challenges positively by collecting information, looking for help, making responsible choices, and taking action	
d) to recognise, as they approach puberty, how people's emotions change at that time and how to deal with their feelings towards themselves, their family and others in a positive way	
e) about the range of jobs carried out by people they know, and to understand how they can develop skills to make their own contribution in the future	
f) to look after their money and realise that future wants and needs may be met through saving	

2. Preparing to play an active role as citizens

a) to research, discuss and debate topical issues, problems and events	
b) why and how rules and laws are made and enforced, why different rules are needed in different situations and how to take part in making and changing rules	
c) to realise the consequences of anti-social and aggressive behaviours, such as bullying and racism, on individuals and communities	
d) that there are different kinds of responsibilities, rights and duties at home, at school and in the community, and that these can sometimes conflict with each other	

e) to reflect on spiritual, moral, social, and cultural issues, using imagination to understand other people's experiences	
f) to resolve differences by looking at alternatives, making decisions and explaining choices	
g) what democracy is, and about the basic institutions that support it locally and nationally	
h) to recognise the role of voluntary, community and pressure groups	
i) to appreciate the range of national, regional, religious and ethnic identities in the United Kingdom	
j) that resources can be allocated in different ways and that these economic choices affect individuals, communities and the sustainability of the environment	
k) to explore how the media present information	

3. Developing a healthy, safer lifestyle

a) what makes a healthy lifestyle, including the benefits of exercise and healthy eating, what affects mental health, and how to make informed choices	
b) that bacteria and viruses can affect health and that following simple, safe routines can reduce their spread	
c) about how the body changes as they approach puberty	
d) which commonly available substances and drugs are legal and illegal, their effects and risks	
e) to recognise the different risks in different situations and then decide how to behave responsibly, including sensible road use, and judging what kind of physical contact is acceptable or unacceptable	

f) that pressure to behave in an unacceptable or risky way can come from a variety of sources, including people they know, and how to ask for help and use basic techniques for resisting pressure to do wrong	
g) school rules about health and safety, basic emergency aid procedures and where to get help	

4. Developing good relationships and respecting the differences between people

a) that their actions affect themselves and others, to care about other people's feelings and to try to see things from their points of view	
b) to think about the lives of people living in other places and times, and people with different values and customs	
c) to be aware of different types of relationship, including marriage and those between friends and families, and to develop the skills to be effective in relationships	
d) to realise the nature and consequences of racism, teasing, bullying and aggressive behaviours, and how to respond to them and ask for help	
e) to recognise and challenge stereotypes	
f) that differences and similarities between people arise from a number of factors, including cultural, ethnic, racial and religious diversity, gender and disability	
g) where individuals, families and groups can get help and support	

Key Stage 3 Citizenship

1. Knowledge and understanding about becoming informed citizens

a) Rights and responsibilities the legal and human rights and responsibilities underpinning society, basic aspects of the criminal justice system, and how both relate to young people	
b) Diversity and identity the diversity of national, regional, religious and ethnic identities in the United Kingdom and the need for mutual respect and understanding	
c) Public services central and local government, the public services they offer and how they are financed, and the opportunities to contribute	
d) Government the key characteristics of parliamentary and other forms of government	
e) Voting and elections the electoral system and the importance of voting	
f) Community and voluntary groups the work of community-based, national and international voluntary groups	
g) Conflict resolution the importance of resolving conflict fairly	
h) Media the significance of the media in society	
i) Global community and environmental issues the world as a global community, and the political, economic, environmental and social implications of this, and the role of the European Union, the Commonwealth and the United Nations	

2. Developing skills of enquiry and communication

a) think about topical political, spiritual, moral, social and cultural issues, problems and events by analysing information and its sources, including ICT-based sources	
b) justify orally and in writing a personal opinion about such issues, problems or events	
c) contribute to group and exploratory class discussions, and take part in debates	

3. Developing skills of participation and responsible action

a) use their imagination to consider other people's experiences and be able to think about, express and explain views that are not their own	
b) negotiate, decide and take part responsibly in both school and community-based activities	
c) reflect on the process of participating	

Key Stage 4 Citizenship

1. Knowledge and understanding about becoming informed citizens

a) and h) Rights and responsibilities • the legal and human rights and responsibilities underpinning society and how they relate to citizens, including the role and operation of the criminal and civil justice systems • the rights and responsibilities of consumers, employers and employees	
b) Diversity and identity the origins and implications of the diverse national, regional, religious and ethnic identities in the United Kingdom and the need for mutual respect and understanding	
c) Government the work of parliament, the government and the courts in making and shaping the law	
d) Voting and elections the importance of playing an active part in democratic and electoral processes	
e) Economy how the economy functions, including the role of business and financial services	
f) Community and voluntary groups the opportunities for individuals and voluntary groups to bring about social change locally, nationally, in Europe and internationally	
g) Media the importance of a free press, and the media's role in society, including the internet, in providing information and affecting opinion	
i) and j) Global community and environmental issues • the United Kingdom's relations in Europe, including the European Union, and relations with the Commonwealth and the United Nations • the wider issues and challenges of global interdependence and responsibility, including sustainable development and Local Agenda 21	

2. Developing skills of enquiry and communication

a) research a topical political, spiritual, moral, social or cultural issue, problem or event by analysing information from different sources, including ICT-based sources, showing an awareness of the use and abuse of statistics	
b) express, justify and defend orally and in writing a personal opinion about such issues, problems or events	
c) contribute to group and exploratory class discussions, and take part in formal debates	

3. Developing skills of participation and responsible action

a) use their imagination to consider other people's experiences and be able to think about, express, explain and critically evaluate views that are not their own	
b) negotiate, decide and take part responsibly in school and community-based activities	
c) reflect on the process of participating	

Useful websites

DfES and QCA sites

www.standards.dfes.gov.uk/schemes

DfES/QCA Schemes of work with direct links to Citizenship schemes of work.

www.dfes.gov.uk/citizenship

DfES Citizenship site

http://www.qca.org.uk/ca/subjects/citizenship

QCA Citizenship site. Includes links to schemes of work; Citizenship and PSHE Updates.

http://www.dfes.gov.uk/progfile/

Progress File is a set of guidance and working materials to help young people from age 13 and adults to record, review and present their achievements, set goals and make progression in learning and in work. A ring binder and presentation folder is available to help young people keep their materials together.

ASDAN

www.asdan.co.uk

ASDAN (Award Scheme Development and Accreditation Network) is an approved awarding body offering a number of programmes and qualifications to develop life skills, from Key Stage 3 through to adult life, from preparatory to Entry Level through to Key Skills at level 4.

BBC

www.bbc.co.uk/education/id

This is the **ID: Learning to be you** section of the BBC website. On the theme of Citizenship, this includes interactive stories with decision-making points along the way. Issues include finding out about communities, recycling, helping others, making decisions and being responsible.

http://www.bbc.co.uk/education/schools/getinvolved/

The **Get Involved** section for 11–16-year-olds has photograph and audio stories of students getting involved in local and global issues.

Books Beyond Words

www.rcpsych.ac.uk/publications/bbw

St George's Hospital Medical School and the Royal College of Psychiatrists produce a series of simple stories that look at life events such as bereavement, leaving home, being arrested and speaking up for yourself. This 'Books Beyond Words' series is books with pictures which tell a story but do not have text, and is used to talk through issues in the lives of people (with learning disabilities).

British Council

www.britishcouncil.org/education/schools/index.htm

The British Council promotes the development of an international dimension to the school curriculum. It encourages and supports international partnerships between schools. Part of the site 'Montage plus' is about global internet school projects.

Children and Youth Partnership Foundation

www.cypf.org

The Children and Youth Partnership Foundation publish a resource (free to schools) called *Make a Connection: Lifeskills*. This is a Key Stage 3 life skills teaching resource that promotes the skills, values, understanding and attitudes that underpin the PSHE and Citizenship curriculum. The 42 lessons, designed for mainstream schools, include ideas for inclusive learning. It is divided into three modules: Connecting with Yourself; Connecting with Others; and Connecting with the Community. The lessons can be downloaded from the site and a number of excellent large photographic images are available for support on-line too.

Children of the Earth

www.childrenoftheearth.org

This website has a 'Cool Multimedia' section which includes multimedia presentations on

- recycling
- deforestation
- native American power animals
- the rainforest
- earth day everyday
- saving energy

Children's Rights Alliance for England

http://www.crights.org.uk

A mine of information and advice about children's rights and involving children in decision-making.

Citizen 21

www.citizen21.org.uk/citizenship

Materials to encourage and develop understanding of the political institutions in the United Kingdom and how they work.

Citizenship Foundation

www.citfou.org.uk

Includes some downloadable resources/activity ideas, including some of the stories from the *You, Me and Us!* file (Rowe and Newton 1994).

Community Service Volunteers

www.csv.org.uk

Eco-schools

www.eco-schools.org.uk

Schools can work for an award – bronze award, silver award or green flag. There are useful resources on-line, for example, environmental review checklists. There is also an international programme.

Fairtrade

www.fairtrade.org.uk

This website includes a photo library and some education resources.

Hampshire County Council PSHE and Citizenship site

www.hants.gov.uk/education/ngfl/pseweb

Includes development framework and guidelines for Citizenship.

Hopscotch Publishing

www.hopscotchbooks.com

Growing Up Today series for Key Stage 1 based on fiction books.

Caring for the environment; Looking after ourselves; Understanding feelings; Dealing with problems; Relationships; People and communities.

Institute for Citizenship

www.citizen.org.uk

Contains downloadable resource pack: *Citizenship Education for Young People with Special Educational Needs: A Resource for Teachers of Pupils Aged 11–16 with Severe and Profound and Multiple Learning Difficulties.*

Also contains other downloadable resources, including a number of useful audit forms.

Produces Citizenship Update (secondary) each term which often has sections concerning special educational needs.

Knockevin – People who help us

http://www.knockevin.com/people_who_help_us.htm

Knockevin is a special school for pupils with severe learning difficulties in Ireland. The site demonstrates a multimedia project on people's jobs within school and in the local community. Video clips, photos and sounds of people are incorporated.

London Children's Rights Commissioner

www.londonchildrenscommissioner.org.uk

This is about children's rights in London. The aim is to make London a more child-friendly place, with children's views being heard. They are carrying out projects to improve children's rights in London.

National Children's Bureau

www.ncb.org.uk

Promotes participation and citizenship. Includes specialist organisations: Council for Disabled Children, Drug Education Forum, Sex Education Forum.

OXFAM

www.oxfam.org.uk

www.oxfam.org.uk/coolplanet is the section for pupils and classroom resources for global issues. These include: *Your world, my world* – photographs of children from around the world with information and children's stories linked to the images and suggestions for activities; *Making a meal of it!* – about food issues around the world – photographs, captions and ideas are included; and *The clothes line* – traces the development of a finished garment from the cotton in the field to a UK shop.

http://www.oxfam.org.uk/coolplanet/ontheline/

On the Line was a millennium project which celebrated the diversity of culture in the countries on the zero degree meridian line. The website contains resources on environmental issues, virtual journeys, country by country, and on-line teaching materials.

Save the Children

www.savethechildren.org.uk

This website includes a range of information, resources and ideas.

http://www.savethechildren.org.uk/eyetoeye/

This section is about Palestinian refugees. There are many photos taken by children of life in Palestinian refugee camps. It includes a matching game, matching the appropriate human right to a photograph, e.g. matching the appropriate photograph to 'You have the right to play and relax by doing things like sports, music and drama.' Another section involves an activity matching photos to written descriptions of the articles of the UN Convention on the Rights of the Child.

School Councils UK

www.schoolcouncils.org

Suggestions for setting up and running a school council.

STOMP

www.stomponline.com

Stomp are a music group who use rubbish as musical instruments. Through the website you can play audio and video clips. There are ideas for activities – for example making instruments, noise v. sound and a rainforest section.

UNICEF UK's youth rights

http://www.therightssite.org.uk/

Includes information about children's rights and a pictorial card game to distinguish wants from needs. Also information and games about different issues – for example clean water and sanitation, food and nutrition and child labour.

Trans-active

www.trans-active.org.uk

Multimedia project supported by MENCAP. Young people with learning difficulties and peer supporter from mainstream working together. Producing personal multimedia passports.

WaterAid

www.wateraid.org.uk

WaterAid is a UK charity dedicated exclusively to the provision of safe domestic water, sanitation and hygiene education to the world's poorest people. The Learnzone section of the website includes activity ideas and resources.

Widgit – rainforest

http://www.widgit.com/html/products/rainforest.htm

This is one section of the widgit site, software symbols used by many students with learning difficulties. This section of the site explores issues concerned with the rainforest in Costa Rica and sustainability, through symbols and photographs.

Wired for Health

www.wiredforhealth.gov.uk

National Healthy School Standard site.

Young Enterprise

www.young-enterprise.org.uk

This includes Primary programmes and Team Enterprise for young people with learning difficulties.

References

Abbott, E. (2000) *Preparing Successful Healthy Educated Citizens: A Primary Teacher's Guide to Implementing the PSHEC Curriculum.* London: educaRI.

ACCAC (2000) (Qualifications, Curriculum and Assessment Authority for Wales) *Personal and Social Education Framework.* Cardiff: ACCAC.

Association for Citizenship Teaching (2001) *Preparing for Citizenship* (CD Rom). London: ACT.

Brown, D. (2000) 'Implementing citizenship education in a primary school', in A. Osler (ed.) *Citizenship and Democracy in Schools: Diversity, Identity, Equality.* Stoke-on-Trent: Trentham Books.

Brown, E. (1996) *Religious Education for All.* London: David Fulton Publishers.

Campbell, J. (2000) 'Assessing citizenship: opportunities and challenges', *Citizenship Update* (Secondary), p.4. London: Institute for Citizenship.

Claire, H. (2001) *Not Aliens: Primary School Children and the Citizenship/PSHE curriculum.* Stoke-on-Trent: Trentham Books.

Clay, D. (2000) *Primary School Councils Toolkit.* London: School Councils UK.

Clough, N. and Holden, C. (2002) *Education for Citizenship: Ideas and Action.* London: RoutledgeFalmer.

Cunningham, J. (2000) 'Democratic practice in a secondary school', in A. Osler (ed.) *Citizenship and Democracy in Schools: Diversity, Identity, Equality.* Stoke-on-Trent: Trentham Books.

Curry, M. and Bromfield, C. (1994) *Personal and Social Education for Primary Schools through Circle Time.* Tamworth: NASEN.

Dale, P. (1997) *Big Brother, Little Brother.* London: Walker Books.

Davies, I. (1996) 'Education for citizenship', in R. Webb (ed.) *Cross-curricular Primary Practice: Taking a Leadership Role.* London: Falmer.

Davies, L. (1999) *School Councils and Pupil Exclusions.* London: School Councils UK.

DfEE/QCA (1999a) *The National Curriculum: Handbook for Primary Teachers in England* (Key Stages 1 and 2) (QCA/99/457) (Also available at www.nc.uk.net)

DfEE/QCA (1999b) *The National Curriculum: Handbook for Secondary Teachers in England* (Key Stages 3 and 4) (QCA/99/458). (Also available at www.nc.uk.net)

DfEE (1999c) *National Healthy School Standard: Getting Started.* Nottingham: DfEE.

DfEE (1999d) *National Healthy School Standard: Guidance.* Nottingham: DfEE.

DfEE (2000a) *Careers Education in the New Curriculum: Its Relationship to PSHE and Citizenship at Key Stages 3 and 4* (DfEE 0039/2000).

DfEE (2000b) *Developing a Global Dimension in the School Curriculum* (DfEE 0115/2000).

DfEE (2000c) *Financial Capability through Personal Finance Education KS1&2* (DfEE 0160/2000).

DfEE (2000d) *Financial Capability through Personal Finance Education KS3&4* (DfEE 0161/2000).

DfES (2001a) *First Impressions: Career-related Learning in Primary Schools* (DfES 0061/2001).

DfES (2001b) *Living Our lives: The National Strategy for Improving Adult Literacy and Numeracy Skills.* London: DfES.

DfES (2001c) *Self-Advocacy Action Pack (Skills for Life: The National Strategy for Improving Adult Literacy and Numeracy Skills).* Nottingham: DfES.

DoH (2001) *Valuing People A New Strategy for Learning Disability in the 21st Century.* CM 5086. London: The Stationery Office.

Dyer, S. (2001) *Five Little Fiends.* London: Bloomsbury Publishing.

Education through Music (1994) *Education Through Music: Exploring Geography.* Coventry: Education through Music.

Fergusson, A. (2001) 'Citizenship: the challenge!', *SLD Experience,* **29**, 10–11.

Fergusson, A. (2002) 'Developing citizen education', *SLD Experience,* **32**, 2–5.

Further Education Funding Council (2000) *Citizenship for 16–19-year-olds in Education and Training.* Report of the advisory group. Coventry: FEFC.

Gold, J. and Gold, T. (1998) *Citizens from the Classroom: Learning by Doing.* London: School Councils UK.

Gregory, P. (2002) 'Making choices', Key Stage 1 Resource, *Guardian Education,* 17 September.

Griffiths, M. (1994) *Transition to Adulthood.* London: David Fulton Publishers.

Grimwade, K., Jackson, E., Reid, A. and Smith, M. (2000) *Geography and the New Agenda: Citizenship, PSHE and Sustainable Development in the Primary Curriculum.* Sheffield: Geographical Association.

Hart, R. (1992) *Children's Participation: From Tokenism to Citizenship.* Innocenti essays No. 4. Florence: UNICEF/International Child Development Centre.

Hicks, D. (2001) *Citizenship for the Future: A Practical Classroom Guide.* Godalming: WWF-UK.

Hill, L. (2001) *Connecting Kids: Exploring Diversity Together.* Canada: New Society Publishers.

Hoffman, M. (1991) *Amazing Grace.* Frances Lincoln.

Holden, C. and Clough, N. (1998) 'The child carried on the back does not know the length of the road: the teacher's role in assisting participation', in C. Holden and N. Clough (eds) *Children as Citizens: Education for Participation.* London: Jessica Kingsley.

Institute for Citizenship (2002) *Citizenship Education for Young People with Special Educational Needs: A Resource for Teachers of Pupils Aged 11–16 with Severe and*

Profound and Multiple Learning Difficulties (CD Rom). London: Institute for Citizenship. (Also available at www.citizen.org.uk/education/senresources.html)

Jerome, L. and Newman Turner, A. (2001) *Activate! Teacher Starter File.* London: Nelson Thornes/Institute for Citizenship.

Johns, R., Scott, L. and Bliss, J. (2001) *Let's Do It: Creative Activities for Sex Education for Young People with Learning Disabilities.* Bledlow Ridge: Image in Action.

Kerr, D. (2000) 'An international comparison', in D. Lawton, J. Cairns and R. Gardner (eds) *Education for Citizenship.* London: Continuum.

Klein, R. (2001) *Citizens by Right: Citizenship Education in Primary Schools.* Stoke-on-Trent: Trentham Books/Save the Children.

Law, B. (2000) 'For richer? For poorer? For worker? – For citizen!', in R. Best (ed.) *Education for Spiritual, Moral, Social and Cultural Development.* London: Continuum.

Lawson, H. (1998) *Practical Record Keeping: Development and Resource Material for Staff Working with Pupils with Special Educational Needs* (2nd edn). London: David Fulton Publishers.

Lawson, H. and Fergusson, A. (2001) 'PSHE and citizenship', in B. Carpenter, R. Ashdown and K. Bovair (eds) *Enabling Access: Effective Teaching and Learning for Pupils with Learning Difficulties* (2nd edn). London: David Fulton Publishers.

Lawson, H., Marvin, C. and Pratt, A. (2001) 'Planning, teaching and assessing the curriculum for pupils with learning difficulties: an introduction and overview', *Support for Learning.* **16**(4), 162–7.

Lawton, D. (2000) 'Overview: citizenship education in context', in D. Lawton, J. Cairns and R. Gardner (eds) *Education for Citizenship.* London: Continuum.

Lees, J. and Plant, S. (2000) *Passport: A Framework for Personal and Social Development.* London: Calouste Gulbenkian Foundation.

McInnes, J. M. and Treffrey, J. A. (1982) *Deaf-blind Infants and Children.* Toronto: University of Toronto Press.

McKee, D. (1978) *Tusk Tusk.* London: Anderson Press.

McKee, D. (1980) *Not Now Bernard.* London: Arrow.

McLaughlin, C. and Byers, R. (2001) *Personal and Social Development for All.* London: David Fulton Publishers.

Macpherson of Cluny, Sir William (1999) *The Stephen Lawrence Inquiry* (The Macpherson Report, CM 4262 – 1. London: The Stationery Office.

Miller, J. (1997) *Never Too Young: How Young Children Can Take Responsibility and Make Decisions.* London: National Early Years Network/Save the Children Fund.

Mitchell, R. and Ayliffe, A. (1998) *The Gotcha Smile.* Orchard.

Mittler, P. (2000) *Working Towards Inclusive Education: Social Contexts.* London: David Fulton Publishers.

National Curriculum Council (1990) *Curriculum Guidance 8: Education for Citizenship.* York: NCC.

Ofsted (2002) *Survey Report: Preparation for the Introduction of Citizenship in*

Secondary Schools 2001–2002. London: OFSTED (HMI 730 E-publication). (Available at www.ofsted.gov.uk)

Ord, W. (2002) 'A change for the better', *TES Teacher*, 24 May, p. 25.

Otten, L. (ed.) (1999) *A Curriculum for Personal and Social Education.* London: David Fulton Publishers.

Otorepec, R. (2002) 'Making connections', *Eye Contact*, **33**, summer, 31–2.

Owen, R. P. and Tarr, J. (1998) 'The voice of young people with disability', in C. Holden and N. Clough (eds) *Children as Citizens: Education for Participation.* London: Jessica Kingsley.

Oxfam (1997) *A Curriculum for Global Citizenship.* London: OXFAM.

Pfister, M. (1992) *The Rainbow Fish.*

Potter, J. (2002) *Active Citizenship in Schools.* London: Kogan Page.

QCA (1998) *Education for Citizenship and the Teaching of Democracy in Schools* (The Crick Report) (Full report: QCA/98/245; Summary: QCA/98/255).

QCA (2000a) *PSHE and Citizenship at Key Stages 1 and 2: initial guidance for schools* (QCA/00/579).

QCA (2000b) *Citizenship at Key Stages 3 and 4: initial guidance for schools* (QCA/00/581).

QCA (2001a) *Planning, Teaching and Assessing the Curriculum for Pupils with Learning Difficulties: General Guidelines.* (QCA/01/736). (Also available at www.nc.net.uk/ld)

QCA (2001b) *Planning, Teaching and Assessing the Curriculum for Pupils with Learning Difficulties: Developing Skills* (QCA/01/737). (Also available at www.nc.net.uk/ld)

QCA (2001c) *Planning, Teaching and Assessing the Curriculum for Pupils with Learning Difficulties: Personal, Social and Health Education and Citizenship* (QCA/01/749). (Also available at www.nc.net.uk/ld)

QCA (2001e) *Citizenship: a scheme of work for Key Stage 3* (QCA/01/776). (Also available at www.dfes.gov.uk/schemes)

QCA (2002a) *Citizenship: a scheme of work for Key Stage 4* (QCA/02/853). (Also available at www.dfes.gov.uk/schemes)

QCA (2002b) *Citizenship: a scheme of work for Key Stages 1 and 2* (QCA/02/877). (Also available at www.dfes.gov.uk/schemes)

QCA (2002c) *Citizenship at Key Stages 1–4: Guidance on Assessment, Recording and Reporting.* (Available at www.qca.org.uk/citizenship)

Roche, J. (1999) 'Children: rights, participation and citizenship', *Childhood*, **6**(4), 475–93.

Rose, G. (2001) *William and the Guinea-Pig.* London: A & C Black.

Rowe, D. (2001) *Introducing Citizenship: A Handbook for Primary Schools.* London: A & C Black/Citizenship Foundation.

Rowe, D. and Newton, J. (eds) (1994) *You, Me, Us! Social and Moral Responsibility for Primary Schools.* London: The Citizenship Foundation.

Ruddock, J., Wallace, G. and Day, J. (1997) 'Student voices: what can they tell us as "partners in change?"', in K. Stott and V.N. Trafford (eds) *Partners in Change: Shaping the Future.* London: Middlesex University.

Sapon-Shevin, M. (1999) *Because We Can Change the World.* London: Allyn and Bacon.

Save the Children (2002) *Young Citizens: Children as Active Citizens around the World: A Teaching Pack for Key Stage 2.* London: Save the Children.

Scott, L. (1994) *On the Agenda.* London: Image in Action.

Sebba, J., Byers, R. and Rose, R. (1993) *Redefining the Whole Curriculum for Pupils with Learning Difficulties.* London: David Fulton Publishers.

Taylor, M. J. with Johnson, R. (2002) *School Councils: Their Role in Citizenship and Personal and Social Education.* Slough: NFER.

UNICEF (2002) *A Life LIke Mine.* London: Dorling Kindersley, in association with UNICEF.

United Nations (1989) *UN Convention on the Rights of the Child.*

Verhellen, E. (2000) 'Children's rights and education', in A. Osler (ed.) *Citizenship and Democracy in Schools: Diversity, Identity, Equality.* Stoke-on-Trent: Trentham Books.

Walmsley, J. (1991) ' "Talking to top people": some issues relating to the citizenship of people with learning difficulties', *Disability, Handicap and Society* **6**(3), 219–31.

Winup, K. (1994) 'The role of a student committee in promotion of independence among school leavers', in J. Coupe O'Kane and B. Smith (eds) *Taking Control: Enabling People with Learning Difficulties.* London: David Fulton Publishers.

Womack, A.S. (2000) *Citizenship Issues: Assemblies about life.* London: Dactyl Publishing.

Index